THE WOMAN'S CURSE

THE LIES OF SUBMISSION AND THE TRUTH
THAT WILL SET YOU FREE

GINGER TAYLOR

Dedication: I dedicate this book to my sweet husband, Greg, my children and their spouses: Adam and Ashlyn, Jordan and Halle, Amber and Zach, Jonathan, Michael, David and Joshua. I pray this book is a blessing in your lives.

Copyright:

Copyright © 2023 *The Woman's Curse* by Ginger Taylor

Coach: A.C. Babbitt

Editor & Formatter: Sam Wright
Cover Designer: Getcovers.com

All rights reserved under the International and Pan-American Copyright Conventions. No part of this book may be reproduced or transmitted in any form or by any means, electronic or mechanical, including photocopying and recording, or by any information storage and retrieval system, without permission in writing from the publisher, except in brief quotations embodied in critical articles and reviews.

This book is not intended as a substitute for the medical advice of physicians. The reader should regularly consult a physician in matters relating to his/her health, particularly regarding any symptoms that may require diagnosis or medical attention.

Scripture quotations marked (NIV) are taken from the Holy Bible, New International Version®, NIV®. Copyright © 1973, 1978, 1984, 2011 by Biblica, Inc.™ Used by permission of Zondervan. All rights reserved worldwide. www.zondervan.com The "NIV" and "New International Version" are trademarks registered in the United States Patent and Trademark Office by Biblica, Inc.™

Scripture quotations are from the ESV® Bible (The Holy Bible, English Standard Version®), copyright © 2001 by Crossway, a publishing ministry of Good News Publishers. Used with permission. All rights reserved.

Scripture quotations marked (NLT) are taken from the Holy Bible, New Living Translation, copyright © 1996, 2004, 2007 by Tyndale House Foundation. Used by permission of Tyndale House Publishers, Inc., Carol Stream, Illinois 60188. All rights reserved.

http://www.newlivingtranslation.com/

http://www.tyndale.com

Scripture quotations marked "NKJV" are taken from the New King James Version. Copyright © 1982 by Thomas Nelson, Inc. Used by permission. All rights reserved. Bible text from the New King James Version® is not to be reproduced in copies or otherwise by any means except as permitted in writing by Thomas Nelson, Inc., Attn: Bible Rights and Permissions, P.O. Box 141000, Nashville, TN 37214-1000.

http://www.nelsonbibles.com/

Ebook ISBN: 979-8-3507-1009-0

Paperback ISBN: 979-8-9882093-9-3

Hardcover ISBN: 979-8-9882093-0-0

For more information, contact **authorgingertaylor@gmail.com.**

Website: authorgingertaylor.com

Instagram: @authorgingertaylor

Facebook: @authorgingertaylor

Foreword

My first encounter with Ginger Taylor was through a mutual friend. Within the first or second time we had met, she was inviting my family over for dinner at her home. The conversation was easy and engaging and I immediately trusted her as a friend. You will quickly find this book to be engaging in the same way, as though Ginger is sitting in your living room sharing funny stories as well as past trials because she cares for you, personally.

A few years ago, I attended a very informal bible study that Ginger hosted for a group of friends. She led lively discussions about topics that many people shy away from or find too awkward to discuss in front of others. It was evident that she has a passion for helping women and marriages. In this book, she has taken on the topic of submission, which has been perverted in our culture to elicit thoughts of inferiority, lower value, lack of importance, and loss of freedom. Through Scripture, she weaves a clear picture of what our amazing God had in store for us when He designed marriage. And while the book is titled *The Woman's Curse*, you will see the blessings that come from submitting yourself to God and to your husband, as an act of worship and reverence to the Lord.

I spend several hours each week talking with women in my daily clinical practice and through biblical counseling sessions. Marriages are suffering. It is obvious that many women either have never been taught their role or are afraid to embrace it due to some misconceptions. This book presents our helper role as a gift from God that will transform your marriage if you faithfully trust in God's promises. I invite you to lean into submission in a way that you may never have fully understood or trusted before, and watch what God will do to elevate your relationship with your husband!

Jennifer Mills Craddock

Contents

Foreward 7
Introduction: 9
Chapter 1: My Story 13
Chapter 2 Under My Husband 37
Chapter 3 Authority 53
Chapter 4 The Strong-Willed Woman 73
Chapter 5 Umbrella of Protection 85
Chapter 6 Discord in Discipline 95
Chapter 7 The Woman's Role 103
Chapter 8 Expectations 111
Chapter 9 Build Your Husband Up 119
Chapter 10 Free to Obey 127
Chapter 11 Our Ultimate Happiness 137
Chapter 12 Preparation 143
Chapter 13 Divorce 155
Chapter 14 Listening to the Holy Spirit 165
Chapter 15 Women in History 171
Chapter 16 My Final Letter 187
Epilogue 193
Acknowledgements 197
Sources 199
About the Author 202

Introduction:

I struggled for years to be a good wife. I was unaware I wasn't a good wife. I believed I was doing well.

I realized, at some point, that I didn't know what a good wife was. I thought I was a godly wife. I thought by my continuous efforts to read my Bible and do multiple Bible studies that I was growing and becoming this ultimately amazing, godly wife.

I would tell my husband what he needed to do and how he needed to do it, to be a good and godly husband. God finally helped me to understand that being a godly wife was not telling my husband what to do and not trying to make him more godly but to be submissive to him. Additionally, my submission to him would allow God to work in his life and be the man God wants him to be. I needed to get out of the way. I am not God.

Women have good hearts and want to do what is right but have no idea what the truth is about submission. I have moved several times because of the military and my husband's job. Each time I moved, my paths would cross with a new set of friends who needed encouragement in their marriage. I always found that the wife was hungry for the Word of God and was surprised to find out she was fighting a curse.

During my last move, I became friends with a young, married woman who became overly excited about the information I was sharing. I was telling her about submission to her husband and combating the curse.

She said, "You have to write a book!"

I said, "I can't write!"

She said, "I can, and I will help you. Women need to hear this!"

A few days later, I visited another woman and shared this information with her.

She said, "You have to write a book!"

I said, "You're the second person to tell me this in just a few days!"

To give a back story, I had gotten sick three years prior and was undergoing chemo for this illness. I was past due for chemo because of our new move. My illness causes seizures, and the only relief seems to come from chemo. Now that my chemo infusion was late, my seizures were ramping up.

The second woman who told me to write a book had laid hands on me, and my seizures had stopped. I thought, *I need to listen to her!*

I'm not a writer, but I feel like I'm Moses with Aaron (author, A.C. Babbitt), helping me write this book. As I said, I am not a writer. I barely passed English, honestly. I'm a math girl.

Truly, I want to be obedient to the Lord. I went home and told God that if He gave me the words, I would write them down. I woke up every morning with so much information to write down.

At first, I thought I would write this down later because I was tired, but I knew I would probably forget everything as this information was not mine. First, my memory is not that great, considering my health issues. Occasionally, I would go back and read it and say, "Wow! I wrote that!" So, the only credit I can take for this book is that I got up and wrote the book —that I was obedient!

I've been sick for the last three years. Once I started writing, I got much better. If I stop writing the book, will I get sick again? I don't want to find out. I will finish this book.

As an older woman whom the Lord has taught so much, let me teach you what is good!

[3] Likewise, teach the older women to be reverent in the way they live, not to be slanderers or addicted to much wine, but to teach what is good. [4] Then they can urge the younger women to love their husbands and children, [5] to be self-controlled and pure, to be busy at home, to be kind, and to be subject to their husbands, so that no one will malign the word of God.
Titus 2:3-5 (NIV)

I have written this book for the woman who has been radically saved and is a born-again Christian who is actively seeking to become the woman God has called her to be.

I pray this book can help you discover how to become that ultimately amazing, godly wife!

Chapter 1:
My Story

I grew up in a dominant, father-structured family. Watching my dad order my mom around and not seeing his love portrayed outwardly toward her, I made a decision early on - I will never be treated like that!

It was easy, living in the society we live in today, to buy into the "equal union." I had no clue that this type of union doesn't work. Well, maybe it can, but only one partner will be happy… the wife! Isn't that what she wants?

GENESIS AND SUBMISSION

I was married, at twenty-one, to a guy who was not going to let me tell him what to do.

It's funny that when I read the Scripture Genesis 3:16, I never clued into the part he would rule over me!

> *[16] To the woman he said, "I will make your pains in childbearing very severe; with painful labor you will give birth to children. Your desire will be for your husband, and he will rule over you."*
> **Genesis 3:16 (NIV)**

If it would help you to see it in a different version, that might make more sense, here is that Scripture again:

> **[16]** *Then he said to the woman, "I will sharpen the pain of your pregnancy, and in pain you will give birth. And you will desire to control your husband, but he will rule over you."*
> **Genesis 3:16 (NLT)**

Wow! *It is my curse to desire to control my husband!* Understanding that is the first step to derailing the power of the curse! I have read that Scripture for forty years before the Lord brought it to light. I had never read the Scripture in different translations or studied it. Nor did I think it was necessary.

Honestly, the only part of that Scripture I focused on was the sharpening of my pains during childbirth. After having seven children, I knew that was true. However, I have witnessed another woman (one of my daughters-in-law) hardly have any pain during childbirth. That surprised me, as I knew it was part of our curse as women.

However, now that I understand it's not our only curse, I get it. Some women may struggle with one curse more than the other. That's for each woman to answer for herself. I got a double whammy. Yea me!! I get to deal with terrible pains in childbirth (thank God for the epidural) and the desire to control my husband. I should add the overwhelming desire to control my husband.

In all the years I have read that Scripture, I never glanced over it or just read it flippantly. So all I can say is that when it was transcribed, it wasn't written for me to understand the meaning. If I go back to the first Scripture (version cited), I have read it a million times.

[16] To the woman he said, "I will make your pains in childbearing very severe; with painful labor you will give birth to children. Your desire will be for your husband, and he will rule over you."
Genesis 3:16 (NIV)

I know that I saw the Scripture and thought, *yes, I desire my husband and yes, he rules over me*. But at some point...and I will refer to my first marriage here...I did not desire him. I no longer wanted to be with him. So this Scripture no longer held up as a curse for me, in its meaning, I would desire my husband. Something was missing. What was missing was my desire *for my husband's position* - and he would rule over me.

MY PARENTS' AND GRANDPARENTS' MARRIAGES

While talking to my mom about her life, I concluded that my dad had made the decision. He was determined to run the home. And frankly, there would not be any question in the home about it.

My mom always said, "You never saw how kind he (my dad) was behind closed doors." Later on in life, I understood my father and why he was the way he was.

****

I grew up knowing my dad's mom, Theda, "Granny." She was a very strong and overbearing woman. I can recall when I was younger, the way she would speak to my grandfather; not ugly, but not submissive. She was in charge! My grandfather was quiet and kind. He was a hard worker. Mostly, he kept to himself. Keeping out of the way, so he wouldn't have to hear what Grandmother had to say.

Granny had a German mother, Minnie Kinsel, whose husband left them for another woman. He left when Granny was eleven, and her brother, my Uncle Merrill, was five. They nearly starved. As an early teenager, Granny played the piano in bars, to support the family. Her mother went with her.

Tom Minton, my grandfather, was a constant fixture at the bar. He had been divorced but met Granny when he was twenty-three years old and she was sixteen. I am still surprised that her mother let her marry him, but you can guess how much influence her mother had over her.

Tom Minton was a long-suffering, patient, kind, hard-working and neighborly man. He was also a man of very few words. He knew Theda needed to express herself by running things, so he let her take charge of nearly everything.

When he had had enough, there was no discussion. He had the final word any time he wanted it. However, from an outsider's viewpoint, this was not very evident.

****

One Christmas when he was rather intoxicated. Granny gave him a pair of overalls as a gift.

When he opened the box, he declared, "Theda, you know I don't wear zippered overalls!"

She said, "If you don't like them, throw the *fern* thing out of the door!"

He stood up, walked to the door and tossed them out. Then, without comment, returned to his seat.

The next morning, when everyone went into the living room, they wondered if he had, now that he was sober, picked up the overalls? The answer...no, they were exactly where he had tossed them. When Granny got up, she went out and picked them up.

Fast-forward to a couple of years before her death. My mom was sitting across from her on the porch. She was saying something about what she wanted to talk to Tom about when she met him in heaven.

My mom said, "I doubt the first hundred years will include that conversation. He has a much more pressing conversation that he wants to have with you." Granny was puzzled as to what my mom was talking about.

My mom said, "I think the first hundred years, he might sit while you try to explain to him just why you buried him in the new, never before worn, zippered overalls!"

****

I can see how generations of parental actions can affect how we respond to our spouses. However, this does not determine how we ultimately act and how God calls us to act!

I am also not saying that my father was wrong in his actions. He was the man of the home. But as a daughter, he was not aware of the tender heart I had because I came across as a strong-willed girl. So his harshness and abrasiveness came across as unloving. I might have seemed to need it because I was so strong, but my heart was tender. I have no doubt he loved me with all his heart. I simply think he raised this strong girl the best he knew how.

MODELING

I grew up wanting so badly to model. I was six feet tall and begged my mom to put me in modeling school. Eventually, my mom gave in. However, she would not put me in just any modeling school. She decided if she were going to pay for the schooling, then she would pay for the best in town. She sent me to

Ben Shaw School of Modeling. Where I learned how to walk, talk, dress, and put on makeup. This schooling helped me achieve some confidence in myself.

The first thing the modeling agency did was cut off my long hair. Oh, how difficult that was for me to accept, but my hair had to flow as I walked on that stage. They tried to teach me how to speak for commercials. I never quite got the commercials down, but I was not trying to be a commercial model. Besides, I was far too tall for that anyway. I had my sights set on the runway.

This was the first time I can remember boys paying any attention. You might think it would have made me happy, but it made me angry. My thought was, *Oh, you pay attention now that I'm all dolled up but not before?* So, I was not nice to boys. This might have saved me in some respects but made me more disrespectful in other ways.

Before modeling, I had achieved the nicknames "diaper face" and "duck feet," as my face had broken out and my feet were huge. I was a late bloomer with no real shape, so "stick" was another name I had been given. Boys were ruthless! I had built up more animosity toward boys.

However, after modeling school began, I remember returning to school with my fresh haircut, and several guys came right up to me, telling me how great I looked. It never ended after that day. Each day I would have a trail of boys following me in the hallway.

This was so new. I didn't even realize that guys did this to girls.

Soon enough, a senior asked me out and I was excited. He was what most considered "the best-looking guy in school." Until I discovered, two months into our dating, he was selling drugs in school, but that's a whole other story. My father caught wind of the situation before I did and grounded me from dating for the year. It caused more grief between my dad and me. This probably added more anger and resentment about why I would not let a man run my life.

Honestly, had I known what this guy was doing, I would have sent him packing as soon as I found out. So my dad finding out before me and grounding me from dating only made me angry for not trusting me. He never told me why I couldn't see this guy anymore. I had to find out on my own.

Later, I came to find out that my brother had told my dad. So there were two men sticking it to me *per se*.

When I broke up with my boyfriend, it sounded something like this… "I can't see you anymore. I don't know why, but when I figure it out, *I will let you know!*"

I know my dad thought I knew, but I was naive. My brother knew I was clueless. So, I held a little grudge for a while. I can still remember the weekend when I finally found out. I overheard him talking to his girlfriend, and he mentioned my boyfriend with drugs.

I was walking down the hall, and I backed up and said, "Wait, does ——— do drugs?"

He had a friend there who had asked me out for my upcoming birthday.

He said to my brother, "Should we tell her?"

I said, "No, that's ok. You just did!"

So, that is how I found out why I was being punished for dating my school-only boyfriend. I had never actually gone on a date with this guy, as I wasn't allowed until I turned sixteen. I was turning sixteen in a week. My father decided maybe we should wait until I was seventeen to date. I was so mad nobody trusted me with that information. I still don't understand why things were handled the way they were. But maybe to get me to this point. Who knows?

I got several modeling jobs. I remember thinking, *this will be my future.* So much so that I remember walking into class for a test one day. I signed my name at the top of my biology midterm exam and turned it in with the rest of the page blank while thinking, *I don't need this...I will be a model.* Oh boy! I had no idea what the modeling world had in store for me.

At six feet tall, I was a runway model, and one day I showed up for an interview, a.k.a. a "walk." I was one of several hundred other models competing for the job. I got up and strutted my stuff. I got the job! Woohoo! I thought, *Wow, that was impressive. Out of all these girls, I got this job. I am on my way*! However, I didn't realize what was in store for me with this job.

When I showed up for the fashion show, everyone was all in one huge, wide-open dressing room with no curtains to cover us. When modeling, one may not wear undergarments. So, I was changing in front of everyone with no undergarments in a co-ed environment...no thank you! I was modest. I made them set up a table so I could change behind it. This was the end of my modeling career! I wanted nothing to do with changing naked in a co-ed room.

Still, I gained confidence. I learned how to dress, put on makeup, and how to "strut my stuff." A real Christian portrait...uh, no! It was added to my wall against men and my receptiveness to them.

MY FIRST MARRIAGE

When I met my first husband, I was in college.

I saw him from a distance and said to someone, "I want THAT guy!"

Woah! Boy, did I get him! I wasn't seeking the Lord! I was looking at an outside appearance and wanting what I thought I couldn't get!

Ultimately, my first marriage ended, no doubt, from the disrespect I dished out, and I became a single mom of three children.

Early in the marriage, although I belonged to the Lord, I didn't live like it. In the marriage, I gave my life back to the Lord. It was only then that I could give my marriage to the Lord. I became very involved in church, and I taught many classes.

Honestly, I thought I was blameless in the divorce. Not that I hadn't made mistakes early on. But he was leaving me for another woman, and I had been in prayer throughout the year for the Lord to help me with my situation.

Most in the church supported me, but a few confronted me and told me I shouldn't get divorced. I could not blame them for confronting me. It's so true that if there is anything you can do to not get divorced, you should do it. I just looked at them and thought, *How can I fix this problem?* Sometimes, I explained my situation, and they understood. He had left me for another woman.

DATING

Within a year, I was dating again. My pastor set me up with one of his student pastors, who had been divorced. My pastor told him if he dated me, he would date the whole church. This was because

I grew up in the church. My father had been the pastor for seventeen years before this pastor.

We dated for a couple of years. It was a little strained as he kept his distance, trying hard to keep it quiet from the church he was dating me. Oh, but people were much wiser than he wanted them to be. He struggled so much with his divorce and inability to reconcile with his ex-wife. I understood his dilemma. If you can reconcile, you should. I wholeheartedly believed that! We parted ways so he could work out what he needed to work out, and I could move on.

My parents finally set me up with a guy who had never been married and had had no children. I met him, and we began a dating relationship. I liked him. I loved the fact that there weren't any children coming into the relationship.

When I dated my previous boyfriend, it was strained with our children. I recognized how difficult it would be for us to come into a marriage, with two sets of children, from two marriages.

So dating a guy with no children was a breath of fresh air. And I was open to having more children. He came from six children, so I thought, *Wow! I could have a lot of kids.* That sounded kind of exciting. We dated for six months, and he asked my dad for my hand in marriage. I was excited!

About a week later, he picked me up for lunch, which was usual for us, and on the way back from lunch, he told me how much he loved my kids and how he loved this and that. Suddenly, I said to myself, *stop smiling, it's coming! He is going to break up with you!!* And he did. I was shattered. My heart was broken into pieces! I didn't know if I could breathe.

The hope I had been given was gone, and I didn't even know what had happened. He didn't even give me an explanation. I went home and tried to pull myself together. This took months. I cried for several months. I cried myself to sleep and called my mom, daily. But ultimately, I decided the Lord would be my husband. I stopped looking for outside relationships to comfort me and looked to the Lord as my supporter.

COMING BACK TO THE LORD

During this time, my parents talked me into moving closer to them to help me with the kids and to help me recover from my pain. So, I packed my bags and moved three hours to get away from everything I knew and start anew. I bought a new home and began a new job.

I started over, and I honestly had to do some deep soul-searching. *What am I doing?! Why am I dating?! I have three kids. I have a great job. I have a beautiful home. I do not need a man.*

I had to ask myself, *What am I doing bringing different men into my children's lives?* My children were not even nice to them. One of my boys was downright ugly to them. One day, I received a phone call that my children had keyed my boyfriend's car. I really couldn't believe it.

When I brought the children into the room, my middle son spoke up and told me that my four-year-old daughter had done it. When I asked her about it, she explained that my middle son had convinced her to do it.

Two years later, that same son soaked my other boyfriend in the bathroom with the shower head while he was clothed.

How can I keep bringing men around? My middle son was struggling with any man in my life. So I decided, that my husband would be the Lord.

A GIFT FROM GOD

I remember being at church and thinking, *as a divorced woman, I can't serve* (of course, this was not from the Lord). However, the Holy Spirit reminded me I could make people feel welcome. I thought, *Yes! I can make people feel welcome!*

Every Sunday, I would walk around and try to greet everyone in our singles class. I would touch their shoulder or shake their hand and say, "Welcome! It's good to see you. How have you been?" Or "It's been a long time since I've seen you."

After being at the church for about a year... one Sunday, as usual (because I was doing my "service" of making people feel welcome) I walked up to a random guy and said, "Hey, it's good to see you back!"

As I touched his shoulder, a voice spoke whom I believe was the Holy Spirit, saying, "Now you can date him!"

I have never heard an audible voice before or since then. Little did I know, that man felt chills down his spine when I touched him.

I said to myself, "Who is he?"

Well, I hurried home. I was eager to figure out who this guy was. I ran across the street to my neighbor, who knew everything about everyone. Unlike my oblivious self, she seemed to pay attention to people in Sunday School. She had been my best friend for the past year. I asked her who this guy was, at church after describing him to her.

She said, "Ohhhh, that's Dr. Taylor."

I said, "Really, Lord? A doctor?"

I saw a doctor as someone who would tell me what to do. Someone who thought he had authority. I never wanted to date a lawyer, doctor or anyone of this stature.

The next Sunday, I went to church, and there he was, asking to carry my Bible and sitting next to me, throughout the day. I mean, *what is going on? Did the Lord speak to him too?*

I remember the week before this happened, I had been riding in the car with my three children. They were whispering in the back of the car.

I said, "What are y'all whispering about?"

The oldest spoke up. "Well, Mom, we think it's time for you to start dating."

I said, "What?! No, you don't! You're not even nice to the guys I date!"

"Well, Mom, that's when we were younger!" the middle son said.

Haha. Younger! They were eight, ten and eleven years old. Not very old, and it had only been a year. But the Lord was preparing their little hearts.

For the past year, my parents, especially my dad, had been anxious because my dad felt obligated to take care of me. As long as I was single, he felt responsible for me.

Occasionally, if I were eating what he thought was too much, he would say, "You need to work on your body."

I would turn my head around quickly and say, "Dad, I'm not ever getting married again."

He would show a sign of remorse, as he knew that I was sincere in my thoughts. I wasn't dating anyone.

After church that second Sunday, the whole singles group went to lunch. My future husband had made lunch plans. The plans were with a friend and his sponsors from the Air Force Academy. His sponsors went to my church and were why he was visiting.

However, when he discovered the lunch plans for the singles group, he immediately broke his lunch plans, to his friend's surprise. He didn't want me to know he had lunch plans in the first place, so when I invited him to go to lunch with the singles group, he said yes. However, his friend tried to remind him of his previous lunch date while he continuously tried to cut him off without me hearing.

When we went to lunch, "my future husband" sat next to me, and I'm not sure we knew anyone else was in the room. We talked the whole time. I was surprised to learn so much about him.

Then from across the table, one of my friends yells out, "Hey Ginger, did you ever get your TV fixed?"

I said, "No. I worked on it all day yesterday. Took the whole thing apart, but I can't get it to work."

He asked me if I wanted him to come look at it. I said, "Sure."

Sure enough, after lunch, he came by and looked at it. No sound came from the TV. After looking at it, he told me he thought it was a problem with the cable company. The cable company was closed over the weekend, so I had to call them the next day.

He told me to call him and let him know what they said.

I said, "O.K."

The next day, the cable company representative said, "Take the card out of the box and then pop it back in, and it should work."

I did, and my sound came back on. I was overjoyed! "My future-husband" had left me his phone number. Excitedly, I called him to tell him that my television had been fixed and to thank him for his help.

He said, "Great, I'm glad I could help. Want to go on a date Wednesday?"

He started his internship on Monday, and we had our first date on Wednesday. I called my parents. It was now time to find a babysitter for these three kiddos. Hence, I called and asked my mom if they could babysit on Wednesday. They wanted to know all about this guy.

"Well," I told them, "He has never been married. He's a doctor. He graduated from the Air Force academy. [My dad graduated from the Naval Academy] He has no children, and he's a Christian…"

My dad thought, *this is too good to be true.* My dad told my mom, "There is no way this guy was for real."

THE SCAMMERS

Since my dad had been a pastor for seventeen years and later retired as a Director of Missions, he had witnessed many scammers within the churches. Many people had claimed to be people they weren't. Whether it was to get money or to get recognition, he had witnessed so many scammers.

Here's one story. When I was in high school, we had a family friend who came to live with us, while she was attending law school. She was around twenty-two years old and sweet. She stayed in my room, which was difficult because I had never shared a room before and never had a sister. But her mother and my mother were the best of friends growing up, so she was welcomed as part of the family.

Years later, when she was in her thirties, she met a guy and fell in love. He had been in an accident and was waiting for a lawsuit to go through for this accident. Because of the accident, he had a wound on his leg that would not heal. He was constantly battling the healing of the wound but had told her that financially, he was awaiting a huge settlement.

Eventually, they were married, and he would set off to work every day. She got pregnant and was hoping to take off from work with the settlement and his work. However, a paycheck never came. She asked him about his paycheck. He said he was having problems switching over the direct deposit.

Two weeks went by, and still no paycheck. She asked him if she could call his work, and he said he would handle the problem. Well, this continued on for another month, until she discovered he wasn't even going to a job. He was leaving and going to the park every day and just waiting until 5 to come home.

As for the lawsuit, he didn't have a lawsuit either. So, no money would come from that either. She discovered that she had married a homeless man. She was an intelligent woman and had been scammed by this man, now her husband.

****

Here's another story. Another fellow at my father's church claimed to have received the Medal of Honor. He was even recognized on the news for it. He would go to the Medical Center every morning, presumably for work. He claimed he was a doctor.

No one was the wiser. However, later we found out that he wasn't a doctor, and he had never received the Medal of Honor.

THE INVESTIGATION

Therefore, knowing this, my father was determined to figure out if my "future husband" was who he said he was. My dad was friends with my pastor and called him and asked him to check this guy out. Then my pastor found my husband's Air Force Academy sponsor, who was a deacon of the church. He sat down with him to ask him about my husband and to find out if he was all he said he was.

The sponsor looked at him and said, "He's a graduate of the Academy! That's all you need to know! Now, tell me about this girl!"

I still chuckle when I think about how crazy all of that was. It was all happening behind the scenes and neither of us knew anything about it.

I went on my first date with him, and at the end of the date, my "future husband" kissed me. It surprised me. I had a strict rule of not kissing on the first date! I asked my "husband to be" why he did that.

He said, "I didn't want you to think this was a friendship thing, and I didn't want to get caught in the "Friendship Zone"!"

Eventually, my "future husband" invited my dad, mom and me for lunch at the hospital. I remember my dad telling me that day, on the way, "We are going to see if he really is a doctor."

I turned to my dad and said, "What are you talking about?"

He said, "We are just going to see!"

In his mind he was thinking, *Why would a guy with all of the things he had going for him, settle for this divorced woman with children?*

My "future husband" would tell you, "It was the Lord!"

MY SECOND MARRIAGE

Long story short, we were married in six months.

I was thirty-three years old, and he wanted to have children. Deciding when to get pregnant was probably our hardest decision. He wanted to wait a few months. However, I was thirty-three years old and didn't want to wait or go on "the pill." I wasn't getting any younger. My thought was *if we will have children, then let's do it.*

Little did I know I would have problems in my pregnancy. I was older. I had never had issues before, so I wasn't expecting problems this time. I had my period on my honeymoon, so I got pregnant right after we married. My husband was a great cook, and I was eating differently than before. I was gaining weight from the pregnancy, from eating, and I was struggling in the pregnancy overall.

We got married within six months of dating because we wanted to remain pure. Now, I can see how people could think we got married to hide a pregnancy. However, when you're not trying to hide anything, you don't think along those lines.

For his residency program, he had his only two weeks of vacation for the year already scheduled. My husband had picked these weeks before he met me. He couldn't schedule any other time off for at least another six months. During these weeks, he could take off, get married, and go on a honeymoon. Other than that, he had to be in the program for the year.

He talked about getting married at the one-year mark, and I said, "That's fine, just stop coming to see me."

I wanted to make sure our marriage remained pure. Instead, he chose for us to get married at the six-month mark, as he didn't want me to cut him off from seeing me if he chose the one-year mark.

I don't want him to sound as if he didn't want to remain pure. He was pure at our wedding. I know that the longer you date someone, the more difficult it gets. My desire was for our relationship to be pure. I needed that because of my past marriage and to have trust in our relationship.

THE ROCKY ROAD

My husband is kinder than any man has ever been and treats my children as his very own. However, I was struggling with having any feelings whatsoever. I was struggling with the physical connection because he wasn't my type. However, we connected emotionally because he loved me so much and treated me well.

I married him because the Lord told me to. It was the craziest thing in my mind. *If I hadn't married him, would I have been disobedient? Would I have been okay to not marry him?*

Our first few months of marriage were rocky, as I struggled with the question, *What did I do?!* My sweet husband was also thinking, *What did I do?!* It likely didn't help I got pregnant. After a few months, I calmed down and gave in to *let's do this!*

At six months, I was going in for checkups with contractions. My pastor and friends were giving us a hard time, asking us if we were pregnant before we were married? Jokingly, I'm sure. I hope!

So, when everyone gave us a hard time, my husband got very frustrated. We had remained pure, and he hates when people question his ethics.

Eventually, it was three weeks before I was due, so technically, I was full term, and the doctor said, "We need to induce you."

I said, "No way. I have not been married for nine months."

The doctor said, "We cannot keep ignoring this problem."

I said, "Ohhhh, No! We are going to ignore it for one more week."

The next week, I had issues, and the doctor said, "We are going to induce you."

I looked at the clock, and I looked at the calendar, and I said, "Go ahead. There's no way this baby is coming out before my nine-month anniversary."

She just shook her head. I had two hours left before my ninth-month anniversary. So our first child was born on our nine-month anniversary.

I'M THE BOSS

Over the years, I remember so often telling my husband how things would be done, and he was sweet to allow me to do so. I'm sure he was praying to the Lord to get ahold of me. Haha!

With his sweet and kind heart, he wooed me and made me want to be under his authority, but I still was my own person.

For years, I was the primary chauffeur of the cars. My husband told me he let me drive the first ten years of marriage because he became tired of my backseat driving and telling him what to do while he was driving. When I became submissive, my driving days ended, but not much to my disappointment.

I remember being on a road trip, and it was getting late. I was driving. He told me, "We are going to drive for one more hour, and then we are going to stop."

I said, "I'm not tired, I can drive for longer."

He said, "No, we are stopping in an hour!"

I argued one more time and again he told me a little more sternly, "I said we are stopping in an hour!"

I hadn't seen him put his foot down too often, but he was stern on this subject. I didn't argue, but I didn't understand either. I mean, I wasn't tired, and if I am equal to him, why can't I drive? So, we pulled over and stopped in the next hour.

****

Later on, when we had been married for about eight years, I would start a personal Bible study. I had been given a head covering and was looking forward to using it.

> ***[5] But every woman who prays or prophesies with her head uncovered dishonors her head---it is the same as having her head shaved. [6] For if a woman does not cover her head, she might as well have her hair cut off; but if it is a disgrace for a woman to have her hair cut off or her head shaved, then she should cover her head.***
> **1 Corinthians 11:5-6 (NIV)**

I had read this verse and had been given a beautiful prayer shawl. When I went to cover my head, the Holy Spirit said, "Now get on your knees and pray."

I thought, *Well, I could, but I can pray sitting up. I don't understand.* Disobediently, I didn't get on my knees.

Again, the next day, the same thing. And the next and the next and so on for five days.

Until I dropped to my knees and said out loud, "I can get on my knees before you! You are my God!"

He immediately responded, "Now get on your knees before your husband!" Wow! I understood what He had said.

When the Holy Spirit speaks to you, the teaching is so profound. So, here I am, trying to put it into words, in this book. My eyes were opened on that day to so much. Scriptures came to life for me!

Author's Note:

I don't want you to get stuck on the head covering, like I did, for years. So I have added more Scripture for reference, to help understand covering your head.

For years, I had taken the "covering of the head" as a literal meaning. I was stuck on that Scripture, to the point of tears. I was praying to the Lord to help me understand it, as I couldn't believe we would have to cover our heads. Had I kept reading, the Scripture explains the meaning, at the end of the chapter.

[13] Judge for yourselves: Is it proper for a woman to pray to God with her head uncovered? [14] Does not the very nature of things teach you that if a man has long hair, it is a disgrace to him, [15] but that if a woman has long hair, it is her glory? <u>For long hair is given to her as a covering.</u> [16] If anyone wants to be contentious about this, we have no other practice---nor do the churches of God.
1 Corinthians 11:13-16 (NIV)

Chapter 1 - Bible Study Questions

A) Genesis 3:16 (NLT): "He said to the woman, 'I will sharpen the pain of your pregnancy, and in pain you will give birth. And you will desire to control your husband, but he will rule over you.'"

1. Did you know there were two curses?

2. Do you struggle with either curse?

3. Is one curse more difficult than the other for you (maybe you have no pain in childbirth or perhaps it's easy to be submissive)?

B) Today women have taken on the role of being in control of the husband.

1. What areas of your relationship do you try to be in control?

2. Do you see your husband giving in and allowing you to take control in some areas (like when he made me his chauffeur)?

C) I can see how generations of actions by parents can affect how we respond to our spouses. But this does not determine how we ultimately act and how God calls us to act.

1. When you look at your actions, do you recognize your parents and the way they acted?

2. Do you respond the way they responded?

3. What was your mom like?

4. What was your dad like?

D) I can see repeatedly how my past affected how I responded to men. When growing up they treated me badly (called me names). There are so many things that can happen in life that can affect how we feel about men, and therefore affect how we treat our spouse.

1. What have affected your feelings toward men in general?

2. What are actions that may have affected how you treat your husband (remember to keep anything negative about your husband to yourself don't share with a group setting)?

E) The Holy Spirit spoke about getting on my knees before my husband (this was not literal but figurative).

1. How do you think the spirit was leading me?

2. What action can you make to begin this process (you can come back to this at the end)?

Chapter 2
Under My Husband

I had always thought I was under God on one side and my husband was under God on the other side. We were equal. However, my husband is under God, and I am under my husband. He is responsible for the decisions made in the family. I can relax. I need not worry. If I follow his decisions, then I can relax, and I am protected.

OUR PRIME EXAMPLE: SARAH

We can see this illustrated in the life of Sarah in the book of Genesis. I have heard people say that Sarah should have said, "No" to things her husband told her to do. But she is praised in the Bible for her obedience and submission.

> *[5] For this is the way the holy women of the past who put their hope in God used to adorn themselves. They submitted themselves to their own husbands, [6] like Sarah, who obeyed Abraham and called him her lord. You are her daughters if you do what is right and do not give way to fear. ...*
> **1 Peter 3:5-6 (NIV)**

However, if I make decisions contrary to my husband's, then I remove myself from this *umbrella of protection* I have, and then I am responsible for the decisions I have made.

Sarah is both fascinating and a true role model. She and her husband were in a severe famine and needed to go into Egypt.

Abraham looked around and said to her, "Listen, it's obvious these people are not God-fearing and would kill me to get to you if they knew we were married. So, let's just both agree to say we are brother and sister?" I'm sure she was looking around and thought the same. Whether she thought it or not, she listened to him and did what he asked. Don't worry, we will look at the real Bible verses shortly.

It's strange to think that we do not or cannot look outside our American eyes to see that their situation was dangerous. The world was not civilized back then. It's still not civilized in some countries today. Because of our American culture, we can't imagine a situation where one would lie to this magnitude. Well, sit down and hold tight because this ride will get rough!

Well, of course, she was Abraham's half-sister, so it wasn't really a lie. Still, they were still omitting the part they were married. So the Pharaoh took her "to be his wife," as the Scripture says. What does that mean? It means he laid with her. Some people don't want to believe he did. Scripture can be interpreted differently.

If you search the "all-knowing" Google, you will find that many biblical scholars have a problem with this thought. I'm sure they just simply can't believe it! There is a lot of discussion about it. Just let me guide you to the most important point that everyone is missing. She was willing and obedient to her husband.

Therefore, because she was, the Lord had to step in. However, I am not willing to get into a debate on whether Sarah slept with Pharaoh because, honestly, that's not the point. She was willing to go, and he took her. He knew he could have had her, and I believe he did. That is why Pharaoh was so upset!

This is why God punished him. I want you to see where Sarah was. She was willing to be married and willing to go to that marriage bed for her husband's sake. Not only that, remember she was barren. God was protecting her at the time in her infertility.

I will refer to Ray Herman, *D. Min.*, who says,

> Since she was taken to the house of Pharaoh, it implies that Sarai becomes a member of his harem and he later acknowledges that he has taken Sarai as a wife. There is no direct statement as to if Sarai had intercourse with Pharaoh, but "becoming a wife, in these narratives, always implies sexual relations."
> (Herman, Ray, D. Min.) (Borgman, Paul)

His research supports my interpretation of this Scripture:

[18] So Pharaoh summoned Abram. "What have you done to me?" he said. "Why didn't you tell me she was your wife? [19] Why did you say, 'She is my sister,' so that I took her to be my wife? Now then, here is your wife. Take her and go!"
Genesis 12:18-19 (NIV)

All I can say is, wow!! So on top of everything, Sarah allowed that too?! How could she?! After all, she is married!! Well, remember to whom she is being obedient? Her husband!

Thus, who comes to her rescue but the Lord. He sees her and plagues the Pharaoh and his family. The Pharaoh sends her back to her husband with servants, animals, and gifts. This was all on Abraham:

[16] He treated Abram well for her sake, and Abram acquired sheep and cattle, male and female donkeys, male and female servants, and camels. [17] But the Lord inflicted serious diseases on Pharaoh and his household because of Abram's wife Sarai. [18] So Pharaoh summoned Abram. "What have you done to me?" he said. "Why didn't you tell me she was your wife? [19] Why did you say, 'She is my sister,' so that I took her to be my wife? Now then, here is your wife. Take her and go!"
Genesis 12:16-19 (NIV)

The Lord intervened for Sarah because she was obedient to Abraham, and God blessed her. Meanwhile, the Lord judged Egypt through this plague. We will continue to remember that Sarah's womb was closed, protecting her, too. This was so important!

Later, if you know the story, Sarah is visited by angels and was told she will have a child by Abraham (Isaac), and now we know her womb is opened.

[15] God also said to Abraham, "As for Sarai your wife, you are no longer to call her Sarai; her name will be Sarah. [16] I will bless her and will surely give you a son by her. I will bless her so that she will be the mother of nations; kings of peoples will come from her." [17] Abraham fell facedown; he laughed and said to himself, "Will a son be born to a man a hundred years old? Will Sarah bear a child at the age of ninety?"
Genesis 17:15-17 (NIV)

Technically before this point in the Bible, Sarah's name was Sarai. However, to maintain an even flow and try to prevent confusion, I will always refer to her as Sarah. But when God makes the promise to Abraham she will have a child in Chapter 17, both Abraham's and Sarah's names were changed to represent the new covenant established by God between them.

> *[9] "Where is your wife Sarah?" they asked him. "There, in the tent," he said. [10] Then one of them said, "I will surely return to you about this time next year, and Sarah your wife will have a son."*
> **Genesis 18:9-10 (NIV)**

Shortly after their visit, Sarah and Abraham moved again and found themselves in a similar situation as before. Except this time, the Lord prevents anyone from touching Sarah (a.k.a. lying with Sarah). God gave the king a dream, and the king immediately told them to leave and gave them gifts of money, sheep, cattle, and slaves.

> *[1] ... Now Abraham moved on from there into the region of the Negev and lived between Kadesh and Shur. For a while he stayed in Gerar, [2] and there Abraham said of his wife Sarah, "She is my sister." Then Abimelek king of Gerar sent for Sarah and took her. [3] But God came to Abimelek in a dream one night and said to him, "You are as good as dead because of the woman you have taken; she is a married woman."*
> **Genesis 20:1-3 (NIV)**

In this Scripture, it finally became clear that Sarah and Abraham had made the original agreement early on and would tell everyone that they were brother and sister for Abraham's life. He told her this would show her love to him. He confesses this to the king in the following Scripture:

[11] Abraham replied, "I said to myself, 'There is surely no fear of God in this place, and they will kill me because of my wife . [12] Besides, she really is my sister, the daughter of my father though not of my mother; and she became my wife. [13] And when God had me wander from my father's household, I said to her, 'This is how you can show your love to me: Everywhere we go, say of me, 'He is my brother.''
Genesis 20:11-13 (NIV)

What is interesting is that God deliberately protected her, her entire life. Her womb was not supposed to be closed anymore, so God protected her and the promised seed. Sarah relied on God for her protection, not on her own strength. She was obedient to her husband, so the Lord stepped in. What is even more interesting is just how beautiful Sarah must have been. She was old and still very beautiful. I love quoting this Scripture:

[5] For this is the way the holy women of the past who put their hope in God used to adorn themselves. They submitted themselves to their own husbands, [6] like Sarah, who obeyed Abraham and called him her lord. You are her daughters if you do what is right and do not give way to fear.
1 Peter 3:5-6 (NIV)

I often wondered, *What did Sarah do that was noteworthy in the Bible?* Sarah was obedient to her husband. She married the Pharaoh and protected her husband, and she would do it again. Would I be willing to do this?

Oh my, I keep telling myself, *be a wife like Sarah who even called her husband lord.*

To help myself with this, I tried to call my husband lord. It sounded something like this... "Yes lllloooooorrrrrddd"... It was the hardest thing I have ever said! At first, I likely didn't even get the "d" sound out of the word. Eventually, "Yes, lord." Then, in the end, my actions spoke way louder than my words.

Understanding the "protection" I have from obedience to my husband is big. This is how I understand the teaching from the Holy Spirit. *My husband is under God and is responsible for his decisions.* Not me. I don't have to question these decisions he makes. *When I step outside this design and question his decisions and decide not to carry them out, then I am responsible for my decisions.* Woah!!! No, thank you!

This should take a huge burden off of you! Understanding that our husband's the head of us, as Christ is the head of the church, is difficult. Yet, receiving the protection it provides is grace! It's still a choice we have, as women, to receive this protection by accepting our role or not. If we do, then there are blessings to follow. If not, then there will be turmoil — no doubt!

> **[22] Wives, submit yourselves to your own husbands as you do to the Lord. [23] For the husband is the head of the wife as Christ is the head of the church, his body, of which he is the Savior. [24] Now as the church submits to Christ, so also wives should submit to their husbands in everything.**
> **Ephesians 5:22-24 (NIV)**

What is interesting is as women, we are semi-protected in our thoughts. I mean by semi-protected that we don't see a lot of evil in the world. I think, as women, we think that things and people aren't as bad as they are. Men, however, see the world differently. They see evil. This is why Eve was deceived, and Adam was not:

[13] Then the Lord God said to the woman, "What is this you have done?" The woman said, "The serpent deceived me, and I ate."
Genesis 3:13 (NIV)

[12] The man said, "The woman you put here with me---she gave me some fruit from the tree, and I ate it."
Genesis 3:12 (NIV)

Notice, he didn't say he had been deceived. He tried to blame the Lord for who He gave him as a helper. Men recognize danger. They know the evil in the world. As women, we see the world in rose-colored glasses. We mostly believe people are good. We want to believe everyone is good. We can be deceived. What is interesting is that Adam was in the garden with her, as you can see in this next Scripture. He was with her all along:

[6] When the woman saw that the fruit of the tree was good for food and pleasing to the eye, and also desirable for gaining wisdom, she took some and ate it. She also gave some to her husband, <u>who was with her</u>, and he ate it.
Genesis 3:6 (NIV)

I often thought Adam hadn't been around when she was in that garden, being deceived. He was there the whole time. She just convinced him to eat the fruit. He could have stopped the whole thing! Her influence was powerful enough to convince him to sin with her. He knew what he was doing. He was not deceived. Had she not done that, would he have taken a bite?

LET NO ONE COME BETWEEN US

I have seven children, but I have only one daughter out of the seven.

I unintentionally got pregnant with my daughter, by my ex-husband, during our separation. It was during what I thought was the end of my first marriage. I didn't know that I was pregnant with a girl, but I was devastated I had gotten pregnant.

The Lord blessed me with a daughter and a daughter who is beautiful on the inside and out. She wholly loves the Lord. Many of my children love the Lord. I hope all of them do. But when I raised my daughter, I taught her the very things the Lord had laid on my heart.

My daughter met her husband when she was seventeen years old. At nineteen, and in her second year of college, she and her husband got married. I was happy that they were getting married because I wanted her to remain pure before marriage. My fear was that the longer they dated, the harder that would be.

The only thing I didn't anticipate was that one year after marriage, before graduation, she would get pregnant. Her husband asked her to drop out of college. *One class short of graduation?!!* I was freaking out.

I said, "Absolutely not! You are going to finish school!"

She informed me of my teaching to her, and that she must obey her husband. After much argument, I had to agree with her. I was not happy!

She said, "Mom, just pray with me that he changes his mind."

Oh my, all I could think about was all the money we had spent at the University of Florida. Also, how she was one class away from graduating and how none of this made any sense. Well, he changed his mind and told her he would watch the baby, while she took her last class, to finish school. They pulled together and graduated together, with a baby in tow.

Honestly, I was thinking of ways I could change his course of action, like sending him the bill, before she dropped out. Or driving down there to have a discussion with him. Let me count the ways of all the things I was thinking about doing to manipulate the situation, to make him change his mind. None of it was very godly! I will not tell you my first thoughts are perfect. Or that I'm ever perfect. I'm far from it! To judge a big sinner, you have one front and center!

Oh, how much she taught me about butting into her marriage and how I also needed to trust God there. Would I have been so happy had he not changed his mind? Well, I can tell you the Lord blesses obedience. So, even though I don't know how the story would have turned out...my daughter would still be blessed for her obedience.

****

My "handsomest" son (his words) and his girlfriend got pregnant. They decided, after counseling from my parents and me, to get married. However, after the wedding, his mother-in-law started to move her daughter home. They had been living in separate apartments. He was under the impression that they would move into their own apartment when they got married.

Why would two adults move from their own apartments to her mother's house? Her mother wasn't moving her daughter home to have a husband. She was moving her home to be with her daughter and the baby. She didn't care if the husband came or not.

Her mother had been married twice before and had a live-in boyfriend for the past twenty years. She made it clear, at some point, that marriage wasn't important to her, but to my son it was, and now, with a baby on the way, it was very important.

When we talked about them getting married, we didn't know that they would move in with her mother. Really, why would you move in with mom when you originally had your own apartments to begin with?

But her mom was a strong-willed woman, and when she found out that her daughter was pregnant, she was moving back home. What was surprising to all of us, was that her daughter didn't say a word. She was willing to be obedient to her mom but wasn't willing to listen to her husband. He told me he didn't know what to do.

I said, "Pray! And move with her as she is your wife." So, he prayed, and he moved with her.

Within a few months, her mother passed away. My son became fearful. He was fearful his prayer had something to do with her death. I had to reassure him that the Lord is in control and loved her mother, too.

I am sad to say that the marriage did not endure all the heartache and pain.

*****

I have another friend whose daughter was married. Several months into the marriage, the daughter did not want to move to where her husband was moving. Her father offered her a way out and brought her home from the marriage for no other reason. Within the year, a terrible accident occurred, and the father passed away. I never put the two together until a couple of years later. I don't know if the two had anything to do with each other. I know that when two people get married and are before God, we as parents need to step out of the way.

These stories point out the lack of submission can destroy the marriage. As parents, we don't need to get involved or provide an escape route. We need to allow them to be their own entity, as husband and wife. I believe we should always encourage reconciliation. It is not our place as parents to give advice to divorce, in any circumstances. That decision can be made only by the child and in prayer. I am fearful of coming between a marriage…beware!

> *[24] That is why a man leaves his father and mother and is united to his wife, and they become one flesh.*
> **Genesis 2:24 (NIV)**

> *[31] For this reason a man will leave his father and mother and be united to his wife, and the two will become one flesh.*
> **Ephesians 5:31 (NIV)**

> *[6] So they are no longer two, but one flesh. Therefore what God has joined together, let no one separate.*
> **Matthew 19:6 (NIV)**

The husband is the head. Not the father of the husband. Not the father of the wife. The husband!

Remember, it's important to honor the marriage. Especially if it's not your own marriage. There should be a genuine fear of God. Even if people are trying to help fix the situation, they need to pray instead that God will work in the situation. Don't ever try to pull someone out of a marriage.

Try to be an encourager of reconciliation. Remember, marriage is between God and the couple. It has nothing to do with you, even as a parent. Encourage your child to do better if your child is struggling. Pray for them and help them.

The Lord protected Sarah for her obedience, repeatedly. The Bible calls us to be a wife like Sarah. To not have fear and to do what is right and just. Remember, you have protection from the Lord from obedience to your husband.

However, if you are making decisions contrary to your husband's, then you remove yourself from this *umbrella of protection* you have, and then you are responsible for the decisions you have made. Strive to remain under the *umbrella* and be blessed for your obedience.

Chapter 2 - Bible Study Questions

A) I had always thought I was under God on one side, and my husband was under God on the other side, and we were equal.

1. Do you feel this way?

2. Do you think that you are equal spiritually (as far as who is directly under God)?

3. Can you see that you are not supposed to be equal?

B) 1 Peter 3:5-6 (NIV) says, *"[5] For this is the way the holy women of the past who put their hope in God used to adorn themselves. They submitted themselves to their own husbands, [6] like Sarah, who obeyed Abraham and called him her lord. You are her daughters if you do what is right and do not give way to fear. ..."*

1. Can you imagine calling your husband Lord?

2. In what way could you submit yourself to your husband that you do not already do?

3. How can you do what is right, and not give way to fear (In our society referring to obeying our husbands)?

C) When I make decisions contrary to my husband's, then I remove myself from this *umbrella of protection* that I have, and now I am responsible for the decisions that I have made.

1. Can you see the protection God has given you?

2. Does this make it easier for you to be submissive to your husband?

D) Sarah agrees to tell everyone they meet they are brother and sister. And then she is taken into a harem.

1. Can you imagine being obedient to your husband to the point of saying you're his sister and not his wife.

2. How might this story have looked had it been you and not Sarah?

3. What do you think they would have done to your husband if you had confessed it was not your brother (putting yourself in their shoes back in their time)?

4. Was this story a surprise to you?

E) When I step outside God's design and question my husband's decisions and decide not to carry them out, now I am responsible for my decisions.

1. Do you understand what this statement means?

2. Does it take the burden off of you to know you are not responsible?

3. Do you still feel responsible?

4. How can you let go of that feeling of responsibility?

F) Matthew 19:6 (NIV): *"So they are no longer two, but one flesh. Therefore what God has joined together, let no one separate."* The husband is the head. Not the father of the husband. Not the father of the wife. The husband!

1. Can you think of a time when you gave marital advice contrary to staying in the marriage?

2. Do you recognize that outside of your own marriage you don't call the shots?

3. Do you know that you should never willingly try to break a marriage up, but always try to help to put it together?

4. What advice would you give to help someone stay in a marriage?

Chapter 3
Authority

DEALING WITH THE MILITARY

I remember, years ago, being married to my ex-husband, and once, I was separated from him, I had to move. He was military, and we were stationed overseas. The problem was, if we were not living together, then I needed to move back to the U.S. He still had two years remaining on his tour. He was staying, and I was leaving.

I, however, was having problems with the military approving my furniture to move back to the U.S. with me. The rule was that the furniture stayed with the military personnel, not with the spouse. I was adamant I would not leave until all of my furniture was packed up and moved with me.

They threatened me in different ways. Telling me, overall, that I had to leave, and my furniture had to stay in storage overseas. I asked them why my furniture would have to stay.

They said, "Because we have to protect the military personnel."

I asked, "So I have to leave the baby beds, baby toys, and everything?"

"Yes, ma'am," was the response of the young stern military personnel.

"No way," I said.

At the time, I was pregnant with my daughter, and I had a one-year-old and a two-year-old. I could not imagine leaving all of my baby furniture. It didn't even make sense. How could I afford to replace any of it as a single mom? I didn't even know how I would afford to live on my own. Let alone try to figure out how to buy new furniture.

In the end, I waited around for four months before they realized I wasn't going anywhere, and they reluctantly released my belongings. They told me I could fly out, and they would make sure that my things were packed up and shipped out.

I said, "Nope, I'm good!"

I didn't think I could trust them. Therefore, I waited there for them to pack up everything. I slept on the floor with the babies, for several days, without furniture, after they packed it all up. I thought, *There was no way the military would take away my children's furniture.* Really it was my furniture, as most of it I had owned before I came into the marriage.

I would not be in submission to this military group I had not enlisted under. One woman told me I was very stubborn and could cause a lot of problems for my husband. I told her they could do whatever they wanted to him!

*****

Years later, when I married again, my second husband was also in the military. We moved several times. After moving to Alaska, I had my sixth child.

I made my two-week well-child appointment. However, the Airforce group in Alaska had figured out a different way to see their infant patients. One problem they faced was educating their patients. To combat this problem, they decided to hold an educational class before you could go to your doctor's appointment.

Later, I showed up, unaware of this procedure of events. I sat in this class for two hours, learning what to do with a crying baby, how to hold a baby, how to feed a baby, how to deal with a crying baby, reasons a baby cries, and what to expect in the coming months. By the end of two hours, I was irrational in my thoughts. I was angry because they had wasted my time.

Mismanagement of my time is a big issue for me, and it was all I could think about. Above all else, I would have to do this when he is one month old, six months old, eighteen months old, two years old… you get the picture. My mind was blown! I was angry because I felt robbed of taking my children to the doctor. I had determined that there was no way I would sit in a class setting for two hours every time I went to a doctor's visit.

As I sat there, I became very angry. I don't know what I said when I got to the doctor's office, but I was vocal about the big waste of time I had endured. With big crocodile tears, I told them my frustrations.

Unfortunately, they took my frustrations and crying as a cry for help.

They said, "We can get you some help." Oh boy… talk about prodding the tiger!

I said, "Oh, you can? What help would that be? Would you be able to send someone to my house to do my dishes and my laundry? How about helping clean my floors? I mean these are the things I could have done in the past two hours."

As they stood there and looked at me, really not knowing what to say, I replied, "How about let's finish this appointment, so I don't ever have to come back and waste my time!"

They finished the appointment, and I left, never to attend a well-child check-up again. When my husband got home that day, he told me he had received a visit from the head of the pediatric department, to talk to him about the situation.

I told him there wasn't anything to discuss and that I would not return.

He asked me to reconsider. I told him there was no way. Besides, he could take the kids to the appointment and sit in the class if he wanted to waste his time. He explained to me the importance of well-child checkups. He thought it was important for the children to attend their well-child check-ups, so he took the baby to the next appointment.

That was his last appointment, also. He did not think anything was wrong with the class, but it was difficult to sit in a long class learning what you already knew for a well-child check-up. These classes were geared for the mothers and not the fathers. He for sure never asked me to go to another class again. Also, he is a doctor. This class was even more difficult for him to attend.

One of the following Sundays, when I went to church, I was met by one of the Nurse Practitioners who saw my children. He was a good friend of ours. He was well aware of the situation at hand. He told me sometimes in life, we do what we are told.

I quickly cut my eyes at him and said, "Maybe you do as you are told! I, on the other hand, am not you! Therefore, I am not going to just do as I am told. Besides, I am not in the military. I didn't sign up for this!"

I knew he was referring to attending the classes and seeing the doctors. Honestly, it was more than that. I was going to do what I was going to do! This was a waste of my time, and they would not waste my time! I mean, really?! You need to tell a mom of six how to care for a baby?! Really?! For two hours?! Way too long!!

Again, this story is to show you I would not be told what to do by anyone.

MADE TO CHANGE

I still have a hard time in life with these situations. During them, my character comes out. They catch me off guard. I find my husband coaching me often on being a better person. Although I fail often, my greatest success is my receptiveness to his coaching and learning from him. I want to be sweet and kind and soft. That's not really me. I'm a little rough around the edges! I wasn't receptive to being submissive until the Lord got ahold of me.

It is what makes me, me, though, and I feel like I have come a long way. I think it is a cop-out when I hear women tell me they are who they are as if they can't change or won't change because God made them this way.

God made us and calls us to be ever-changing. To be seeking Him and to be trying to become a better person. A mystery, perhaps, but one that can be solved if only we would try to solve it. It is all so interesting! God keeps us on our toes. We will never figure out God; His ways aren't our ways. But we can come closer to Him. The closer we get, the more He makes sense. He is an awesome God! Don't ever stop changing. Keep seeking Him. Grow close to Him.

[22] You were taught, with regard to your former way of life, to put off your old self, which is being corrupted by its deceitful desires; [23] to be made new in the attitude of your minds; [24] and to put on the new self, created to be like God in true righteousness and holiness.
Ephesians 4:22-24 (NIV)

You know, as we live everyday life, as Christians, it's difficult. We are to set an example to a confused world. To a world that has no boundaries. They live under no authority, with no respect for anyone.

REAL-LIFE EXAMPLES

One morning, I sat listening to the news of a woman that went to a school and slapped a school official, and my husband said "We wonder why her child is fighting. Well, we don't wonder. She is setting an example for her children to follow."

Here's the thing. This respect is on such a grander scale than we think.

When I go to a basketball game to watch my children play, I often hear calls I don't agree with. But I have to remember who is in authority on the court. Hence, when I cross the line and argue with the call on the court, I disrespect the referee's position and my children are listening and learning.

Now, he could have missed something. He is human. We often expect these people on the court to be perfect and have perfect eyes. I have even seen one person yell out a wrong call, and everyone jumps on board with him. But when I replayed my video, the referee was correct. I have also seen a wrong call from the referee. Ultimately, we must respect the referee's position and call, whether he was correct or not, because of his position of authority on the court.

This teaches our children that respect is important and that we should respect authority, including our parents. How will they respect their parents if their parents can't respect those in authority?

I was once at a game when across the game, in the stands, a man was so disrespectful to the referees that he was thrown out of the game. Later, I discovered that that man was a referee himself. So again, I must say, we are missing an important lesson in our society, with respect. He couldn't even respect his own kind.

I have to work hard at being respectful when it comes to police officers. However, my husband has always been a good teacher regarding respecting authority.

When I first met my husband, I couldn't stand police officers. My ex-husband was one. It made it very difficult or maybe impossible, in my mind, for me to respect them.

One time, shortly after my divorce, I remember getting pulled over by a police officer. My ex-husband had been on the force for a while, and most of the police officers knew him. I was moving and had a bunch of paperwork in my car, in boxes, because of the move. I'm sure the police officer had no idea why I would have all of these boxes in my car, and I didn't offer any explanation out of irritation for him pulling me over.

When he asked me why I had all the boxes in my car, I simply responded. "None of your business, do you want to write a ticket or not? And we can move on with our own businesses."

This made him observantly angry. Yes, I got a ticket. I'm sure I wouldn't have gotten a ticket had I cooperated. But I thought his question was leading to why is my car messy? Therefore, I took it as rude. I was not receptive to him.

Years later, after I was married and after the Lord had worked on my submissive heart, I was pulled over again. I did not know why I was being pulled over, and I am not one to typically speed or drive erratically, but I remember my ill feelings coming up immediately.

My sweet husband simply looked at me as I pulled the car over and said, "Remember to be respectful. They are simply doing their job. Be kind to him!"

I was obedient to him, and the police officer was kind. I think I had a light out, he gave me a warning, and I immediately had it fixed. He could have given me a ticket. It was in his right to do so. I would have needed to respect that decision. That would have been hard for me.

I pray I continue to change and that I am not caught off-guard, that I will be kind in the future in case I get a ticket. Even if I only have a burnt-out light.

DO WHAT'S RIGHT

We may have a hard time respecting the person in the position of authority because they may be someone we know or knew who made questionable decisions. Or, frankly, maybe we just didn't like them in general. It doesn't matter. I must respect the position of authority. *Remembering the position and the person are separate.*

Although it is sometimes difficult to respect a person, we must always respect the position and trust God. We must also remember to trust those we put in the position of authority as leaders. However, whether they are good or not is not up to us. We must respect them and their positions. To teach our children to respect authority, as it teaches them to respect the Lord and His authority.

So once more, I find myself with the bigger issue in our country concerning the slander of presidents, governors, mayors, etc. Not to mention other people in other offices. Now, I bring this up to show you just how much the Lord has shown me in being obedient and submissive to them.

I stand in front of a flag and say, "I pledge allegiance to the flag of the United States of America and to the Republic for which it stands, one nation under **God**, indivisible, with liberty and justice for all."

See, if I really believed in God, then I would not stress when I go and vote and a person is put into office that I did not vote for. When that person does things that I feel are wrong against this nation, then my God will take care of it.

I see so many people get upset and rise up to attack as if another country has come in and taken over when their politician did not win the vote. I hear of many things that were fraudulent that might have happened. It could have been. But I know that my God is a big God. Although, I'm not saying to lie down. What I am saying is that whoever did get put into office is to be respected. We should pray to ask God to always be transforming our nation into His.

However, it starts here with this change of heart. Also, having an understanding that God uses people in positions to humble His people and to bless His people. As children, we are not always rewarded. *We don't deserve the best all the time!!* I think that if we would get back on our knees and rely on Him, then we could see amazing things happen. I believe this! Of course, we would have to be patient and honest. We would have to be willing to accept whomever the Lord allows, as that may be how He changes things.

As we are impatient in our marriage and want immediate results, we are impatient for seeing God's design. We want to see His immediate blessings. He doesn't always bless immediately. However, by living a life under God and allowing Him to take over, He can put things in order and bless them along the way. Voting to put people in office that should be in office is your right. However, outside of voting, we need to pray for those in office, like we would for our spouses.

DANIEL AND KING NEBUCHADNEZZAR

I often think of Daniel and the lions' den. His story is one of devotion to a man not of God. But Daniel himself loved God. Daniel would have done anything for the king, even though he was not of God:

[19] The king talked with them, and he found none equal to Daniel, Hananiah, Mishael and Azariah; so they entered the king's service. [20] In every matter of wisdom and understanding about which the king questioned them, he found them ten times better than all the magicians and enchanters in his whole kingdom. [21] And Daniel remained there until the first year of King Cyrus.
Daniel 1:19-21 (NIV)

The king had a dream and wanted an interpreter. However, no one knew what the king dreamt. Everyone felt he was asking for the impossible - to tell what the king's dream was and to give an interpretation. The king decided to kill every wise man, enchanted magician, and diviner. But when Daniel discovered this, he prayed and asked God to reveal the dream to him and saved everyone:

> *[26] The king asked Daniel (also called Belteshazzar), "Are you able to tell me what I saw in my dream and interpret it?" [27] Daniel replied, "No wise man, enchanter, magician or diviner can explain to the king the mystery he has asked about, [28] but there is a God in heaven who reveals mysteries. He has shown King Nebuchadnezzar what will happen in days to come. Your dream and the visions that passed through your mind as you were lying in bed are these:*
> **Daniel 2:26-28 (NIV)**

> *[37] Your Majesty, you are the king of kings. The God of heaven has given you dominion and power and might and glory; [38] in your hands he has placed all mankind and the beasts of the field and the birds in the sky. Wherever they live, he has made you ruler over them all. You are that head of gold.*
> **Daniel 2:37-38 (NIV)**

Daniel then interpreted the king's dream, which he had not been told of in the first place. This made it even more miraculous! In return, the king responded:

[46] Then King Nebuchadnezzar fell prostrate before Daniel and paid him honor and ordered that an offering and incense be presented to him. [47] The king said to Daniel, "Surely your God is the God of gods and the Lord of kings and a revealer of mysteries, for you were able to reveal this mystery." [48] Then the king placed Daniel in a high position and lavished many gifts on him. He made him ruler over the entire province of Babylon and placed him in charge of all its wise men.
Daniel 2:46-48 (NIV)

But what does the king do right after this…?

[1] King Nebuchadnezzar made an image of gold, sixty cubits high and six cubits wide, and set it up on the plain of Dura in the province of Babylon. [2] He then summoned the satraps, prefects, governors, advisers, treasurers, judges, magistrates and all the other provincial officials to come to the dedication of the image he had set up. [3] So the satraps, prefects, governors, advisers, treasurers, judges, magistrates and all the other provincial officials assembled for the dedication of the image that King Nebuchadnezzar had set up, and they stood before it. [4] Then the herald loudly proclaimed, "Nations and peoples of every language, this is what you are commanded to do: [5] As soon as you hear the sound of the horn, flute, zither, lyre, harp, pipe and all kinds of music, you must fall down and worship the image of gold that King Nebuchadnezzar has set up."
Daniel 3:1-5 (NIV)

I encourage you to continue reading about Daniel, Shadrach, Meshach and Abednego. How they served under King

Nebuchadnezzar, and how the only thing they did not do was break the commands of the Scripture. They followed what was right.

Some of these rules we as Christians would not have to follow, like abstaining from eating the food they ate. If the Holy Spirit puts it on your heart to abstain from certain foods or drinks, then I encourage you to do so.

Daniel, Shadrach, Meshach and Abednego also refused to bow down to false gods. This happened twice in this story. In the Scripture, both times, God had to step in to rescue them. The first time, he rescued Shadrach, Meshach and Abednego from the fire and the second time, God rescued Daniel from the Lion's mouth. I wonder how hard it was for Daniel to serve under Nebuchadnezzar. Nebuchadnezzar had besieged the King of Judah and robbed the temple of God.

[1] In the third year of the reign of Jehoiakim king of Judah, Nebuchadnezzar king of Babylon came to Jerusalem and besieged it. [2] And the Lord delivered Jehoiakim king of Judah into his hand, along with some of the articles from the temple of God. These he carried off to the temple of his god in Babylonia and put in the treasure house of his god.
Daniel 1:1-2 (NIV)

I could not imagine serving under this king, but not Daniel. He spent time in prayer and not in hostility. He was in submission to the authority of God and King. Through his submissiveness, he allowed the Lord to show miracles and actually get the king's attention at times. I wonder if all too often when trying to do God's work, are we trying to be God, or are we actually praying and seeking His will? Let's let the Scripture here speak for itself:

[1] Let everyone be subject to the governing authorities, for there is no authority except that which God has established. The authorities that exist have been established by God. [2] Consequently, whoever rebels against the authority is rebelling against what God has instituted, and those who do so will bring judgment on themselves. [3] For rulers hold no terror for those who do right, but for those who do wrong. Do you want to be free from fear of the one in authority? Then do what is right and you will be commended. [4] For the one in authority is God's servant for your good. But if you do wrong, be afraid, for rulers do not bear the sword for no reason. They are God's servants, agents of wrath to bring punishment on the wrongdoer. [5] Therefore, it is necessary to submit to the authorities, not only because of possible punishment but also as a matter of conscience. [6] This is also why you pay taxes, for the authorities are God's servants, who give their full time to governing. [7] Give to everyone what you owe them: If you owe taxes, pay taxes; if revenue, then revenue; if respect, then respect; if honor, then honor.
Romans 13:1-7 (NIV)

So as you can see, God has decided, in advance, who will be in authority. When we rebel against who He has put into authority, then the Scripture is clear that we are rebelling against Him. Notice we do not go unpunished for rising up against the authority He has put in charge. My prayer is that you prayerfully consider His Word and do not be deceived by the world and what they present. Do not get wrapped up in things that do not matter. Be convinced that your God is a big God and He is still in control!

POLITICS VS. THE GOSPEL

This has been a heavy burden on my heart regarding how much people try to convince others to vote one way or the other.

As a teenager, I remember so often talking to people about the Lord - it was huge. As a matter of fact, telling people about Jesus and leading them to the Lord was a primary focus in church.

Today, it is hardly talked about. I'm not sure why or what happened. There are more lost people today than ever. We need to be sharing Christ and leading people to the Lord constantly.

Unfortunately, that is not a primary focus today. We want to argue with a Democrat about voting Republican or to a Republican about voting Democrat. Why are we talking about politics today?

Why aren't we sharing about Jesus? You are never going to change someone's mind when it comes to politics. However, if Jesus is Lord of their life, then He will have them vote whichever way the Spirit leads them, and honestly, that is not your concern.

My husband thought I should add that I used to get very wrapped up in politics years ago. So much so it consumed my life to some extent. It's all I could think about until the Lord got ahold of my life. So I am not speaking about it without having experienced the profound need to do something about our politics and try to convince people to vote one way or the other. I want to encourage you, if you are like I was, to pray and ask the Lord to reveal his truths to you. I know that it is so much more important to lead people to him than to sway them to vote a certain way. We are wasting precious time and pushing people away with hate. I would rather them hate me over Jesus than to hate me over a political view. It's just not worth it!

I know this is a hot topic. But it is one in which the Holy Spirit did show me, it was so out of control because of our authority issue. Also because we have lost our focus on leading people to the Lord. Let's get back on track. If you want them to vote for godly things, then lead them to God! Stop talking about politics that won't lead them to God!

Chapter 3 - Bible Study Questions

A) My character comes out during difficult situations. These situations actually catch me off guard. Like when I went to my well-child checkup. I find my husband coaching me often on being a better person. Although I fail often, I find that my greatest success is my receptiveness to his coaching and learning from him. I want to be sweet and kind and soft.

That's not really me. I'm a little rough around the edges!

1. Are you rough around the edges?

2. Can you think of a time when you were surprised and not receptive to authority?

3. Do you think you will be receptive to future coaching from your husband to be under his authority?

4. Do you have something in your life right now that you could give to God and be under His authority?

B) God made us to be ever-changing. He calls us to be ever-changing. To be seeking Him. To be trying to become better. A mystery perhaps that can be solved if we would try to solve it. It is interesting, too. God keeps us on our toes. We will never figure out God; His ways aren't our ways. But we can become closer to Him. The closer we get, the more He makes sense. He is an awesome God. Don't ever stop changing. Keep seeking Him. Grow close to Him.

1. Was there ever a time when you didn't think you needed to change as a Christian (like this is who I am)?

2. Has there been a time in your life when God called you to change a specific area of your life? What was it?

3. Do you feel this chapter has made you want to seek the Lord's authority in your life?

4. How will you make changes in your life? What steps do you think you can take?

C) Sometimes, we may have a hard time respecting the authority of a position because of someone we know or knew who may have been questionable in their actions. Frankly, maybe we didn't like them in general. It doesn't matter. I must respect the position of authority. Remembering the position and the person are separate.

1. Can you think of a person in a job you dislike? Do you have a hard time respecting them and their position (you do not have to name them)?

2. Do you understand that the position and the person are separate?

3. Write a prayer and ask the Lord to help you understand how to be under authority as He calls you to be.

D) Daniel served under what I would consider a terrible king. He was almost killed twice. But he spent time in prayer and not in hostility. He was in submission to the authority of God and King. By being obedient to his authority he allowed the Lord to show the king and others miracles that actually got the king's attention. I wonder if, all too often, we are trying to do God's work. If we are trying to be God.

1. Do we trust God to put who He thinks should be in office?

2. Can God be in control of an office, even if someone is trying to be fraudulent?

3. Does God use leaders to judge His nations?

4. If the people of your nation came back to God, could He heal your nation?

5. Should we ultimately trust God with whomever is in office and be under their authority?

E) When I grew up as a teenager, I remember so often talking to people about the Lord. It was huge. Matter of fact, telling people about Jesus and leading them to the Lord was a primary focus in church. Today it is hardly talked about.

I'm not sure why or what happened. There are more lost people today than ever. We need to be sharing Christ and leading people to the Lord constantly.

1. Do you notice more conversations about politics or about Jesus when talking to lost people?

2. Do you think there is any benefit to arguing about politics?

3. What do you think Jesus would say today about our conversations regarding politics?

4. How can we get back on track and lead people back to the Lord?

5. How can we change our focus from politics to evangelism?

Chapter 4
The Strong-Willed Woman

Obedience is a difficult thing for me. Well, frankly, it's difficult for any woman. It is our curse! But let's just say we give in and buy into wanting to be obedient to our husbands. How far does that obedience go? Well, for me, I'm all in!!

It does not mean I'm perfect! Believe me; I'm a work in progress. There are many reasons obedience is difficult for me. But to start, I am a strong-willed woman. By sharing stories with you, I think maybe you can get a picture of who I was and the very person I am trying to control inside.

REAL-LIFE EXAMPLES

When my daughter was in the fifth grade, she was in the Spelling Bee. I was always at her events, spurring her on and trying to support her. But mostly, I wanted her to have the best opportunities she could have.

When it was her turn to spell, she stepped up to the podium, and the pronouncer gave her a word: "undertow." The room fell silent. Seconds seemed like hours. I sat there and could tell she did not understand what the pronouncer had said. Everyone was silent as a normal spelling bee should be. As my daughter stood there in confusion, I couldn't help but come to her defense.

I stood up and cried out, "Repeat the word again, she doesn't understand!"

All eyes went to me. All I could think about was her not having understood what they had said. I wanted her to have a fair chance. Honestly, my daughter will never forget that moment. She later told me she was embarrassed, but forever grateful to have a mom that comes to her defense. It is actually a fond memory of hers, strangely.

****

Growing up, I was an only daughter, and my dad would put boxing gloves on my brothers when I was four or five years old. I would stand there and beg to box with the boys. I have heard they beat me up. I heard I got knocked out. But my father let me do it and taught me all the while. Though, maybe he didn't let me box after they knocked me out. Haha!

When I was in middle school and high school, my dad would come home from work and play football outside with the boys, and sure enough, I was out there playing with them. My dad was the all-time quarterback.

He would tell us, "Absolutely no tackle football."

So when we played with dad, we played touch football. When dad wasn't around, though, it was full-on knock-down, drag-out, tackle football. I was good at the clothesline move. I would hang their neck with my arm as they ran by me, and down they went. I was that rough-and-tough girl. Believe it or not, when the boys picked their teams, I was not the last one to be picked, probably due to my clothesline move!

****

Growing up, I went to school in an inner-city middle school and high school in Houston, Texas. I was involved in many fights. I was taught not to start a fight but to finish it (after being beaten up in sixth grade from not fighting)!

As I went to school one day, I could hear whispering in the halls that the meanest, toughest girl in school would beat me up. I thought, W*ell, if I ignore it, it won't happen.* She actually rode on my bus. She was in the eighth grade, and I was in the sixth grade. I wasn't scared because I just didn't think it would happen.

When we got to her bus stop, everyone looked over to see whether they would exit the bus. It all depended on whether she stayed on the bus. She didn't get off the bus. Neither did anyone else. Talk about a packed bus!

As my delusional self, I continued to think I would be okay with my plan at hand. Just walk away! I mean, I still had no reason to fight her, so it would not happen. How can anyone get enough rage to fight someone for no reason? Later on, I found out there was a reason, and it was because of a fight I had had with a different girl. She was coming to her defense.

When we got to my bus stop, she and everyone else on the bus got off. Everyone wanted to see this fight. It was going to be a good fight. Little did they know that I wasn't going to be much of a fighter. I turned to walk away, and the next thing I knew I was being awoken. She had knocked me out and beat me so badly that I almost needed hospital care. Had the neighbors not come out and stopped it, no telling what would have happened.

When we got home, my father was furious. He asked my brother, who was on the bus with me, why he didn't step in to rescue me. He said the other guys had threatened him and told him they would beat him up if he stepped in. There were likely fifteen guys standing there that were a year older than him. I can envision John Travolta in *Grease*, with his gang, ready to pounce.

My dad let him know that he didn't have to worry about those boys hurting him. He would have to worry about his dad if he ever came home after standing there and watching his sister get beat up again. As a matter of fact, he might just not want to come home.

You might say I didn't lose a fight after that one, and the one fight I could have lost, my brother jumped over about four seats in the bus to join me in the fight.

He later told me he could remember dad telling him he "better not come home if your sister gets beat up again on your watch."

I was one tough cookie. Most fights I was in were in middle school. I didn't have anyone bother me in high school.

I wasn't one to start a fight. I would tell them, "I would be okay to finish it, though."

****

Shortly after my divorce, I was struggling to make ends meet. I was not receiving steady child support for the first couple of years. The kids and I would often go on bike rides together. I had bought each child new bikes, and they had left them outside.

One morning, I looked out my window to see men loading my children's bikes into their pickup truck. Panic struck me, as I knew I couldn't afford to buy them new ones. I wasn't even dressed yet. I quickly dressed and gathered the kids, and loaded them in the car to fearlessly chase after the pickup truck.

As I followed him, I noticed he was obviously looking for items being left outside to load into his truck bed. I continued to follow close behind, and I watched him load items into his truck from several houses. While he was pulled over at one of those homes, I demanded my bikes back. He was a rough-looking guy that likely wondered why this young woman would have followed him. After a small argument and a threat of calling the police, he reluctantly gave me my bikes back.

****

When my son was stationed in Hawaii, he needed surgery. My mother and I flew to Hawaii to help take care of him.

One morning, before his surgery, as we were sleeping in his living room on his futon couch, my mom woke me, whispering someone was breaking in. I jumped up and ran to the door. I saw a man at the door.

It was around 4:30 am, so it was dark. He had a hoodie on. His head was down, and he was messing with the door. I could see him through the glass pane of the door. I quickly made a plan, not a long and difficult plan. But I made a plan: scare him!

So, I banged loudly on the front door and yelled, "WHAT ARE YOU DOING?!"

The man quickly looked up, and as his eyes met mine, I realized it was my son. He had left to take another military person to work at 4:00 am that morning.

My mom said, "What is *wrong* with you! I wanted to hide under the couch!"

However, my instinct was not to hide under the couch but to protect everyone in the house. I thought, *Perhaps I could scare him, and he might run away!*

****

We moved to Florida when my daughter was sixteen and bought a property with two homes on it. There was a small, one-bedroom efficiency apartment behind our home. I thought it would be a great idea to fix the home up for my parents, to come and stay with us on occasions when they came to visit.

Once we remodeled it, I called my mom, and she recommended that I let my daughter live in it. She said it would be a shame to let it sit empty and that my daughter needed her privacy as she was starting college that year. She had been accepted at Collegiate High School of Northwest Florida State College.

I was reluctant because she was sixteen. But I ended up agreeing to let her live there. I understood she needed privacy from all her little brothers. It seemed perfect, after my mother described how much quiet and privacy she would need to study.

"And besides," my mom said, "It's just behind your house."

One night, my daughter called me to tell me she heard something outside her door. I was "patiently" waiting for my husband to open the safe to get the gun. However, it seemed like he was taking too long (like an eternity in my head, though it was likely only a few seconds), and my daughter's safety was all I could think about.

I could imagine what all was happening in the time he was taking to open this safe. She's only 16; she's a fragile flower! I could only imagine killing whomever this crazy person was that would come between this mama bear and her cub! So, off I went out the door. I set out to tackle the intruder and protect my daughter.

Later that night, my husband said, "You could have been killed!"

I said, "I was willing to die, and then you could have killed him, and my daughter would still be safe. I would have surprised the intruder and slowed him down." He just rolled his eyes.

****

My son was having issues in a class in middle school. I went to the teacher to talk to her and to try to resolve the problems. She told me he was not turning in his homework. I asked her to give me all of his assignments and that I would make sure they were turned in. So she gave them to me.

That weekend, I made him complete all of his assignments and turn them in. When he came home from school, I asked him if he had turned them in.

He said, "I did, but she wadded them up in front of my face and threw them away!"

Oh my!! All I could think was.... *I DON'T THINK SO....* I mean, I had gone to the teacher and spoken to her, and she gave me the assignments. *So how can you give them and then throw them away like that...wad them up in his face and throw them away?!*

I went to the principal and asked him to be transferred out of her class. He asked if I had spoken to the teacher.

I said, "I'm speaking to you!"

He said, "Well, we can have all his teachers come."

I said, "There is no need for that." *Was he trying to turn everyone against my son?* He scheduled the meeting.

That next day, I got a call from a different teacher saying, "I don't know what your son tells you, but he did *such and such* in my class."

I told her, "He actually tells me nothing, but I think at this point, you can come to the meeting, too."

I knew that somehow these two teachers were talking about him to each other. I wasn't sure what was being said, but what I was sure about was that it was a one-sided conversation from the perspective of that original teacher, who wadded his homework up in his face.

When I showed up for the meeting, all of his teachers were there. I dismissed them all, to the principal's dismay, except for the two I felt were causing problems.

The principal asked, "Where should we begin?" and when I spoke up, the principal said, "I'm speaking to him," and shut me up and pointed to my husband.

I was boiling! I was so angry with the principal for being disrespectful and rude. I was angry with my husband for not defending me. Still, by the end of the meeting, my son was transferred out of her class, and the other teacher who had called me apologized after hearing what my son had gone through.

When I got to the car, I asked my husband why he did not stand up for me. He said, "We got what we wanted. I did not think this meeting was about us." I agreed with him, but I was not happy.

BEING FULFILLED

I am a strong-willed woman. So being under a man was definitely the last thing I ever thought I would be doing in life. But what an amazing adventure, and so fulfilling.

I wonder if you can relate to being a strong-willed woman when you read these stories? I share them to tell you that my life is fulfilled in my submissiveness to God under my husband. All the things that my heart desires for my husband are met by being submissive to him.

WHAT YOU SHOULD ALWAYS SAY YES TO

One lesson I taught my daughter, and my mother taught me, was to never tell our husbands no in the bedroom. So, regarding sexual relations in our home, unless I was on my period, I did not tell my husband no. This is very important. Men need to know that they have a safe place to come and not be told no when they have a need. If you have a headache, we have medicines for that. Get that taken care of early, and always be prepared for when your husband is in need.

It has been brought to my attention that sometimes the wife desires sex more than the husband. With sexual relations, there can be many reasons a spouse can be turned off. One reason a partner might be turned off is because of cleanliness.

I have a rule of thumb: we both go to bed clean. I like a clean bed. This allows us to be able to have intimacy anytime we go to bed and for cleanliness not to be a factor. If it is a factor for you as a woman, then I would encourage you to talk to your husband about your desires regarding going to bed clean. If you're not sure how to approach him, then seek professional counseling.

We should always try to talk to our spouse and come to an understanding of what works with both partners so there are no frustrations. Talking is important.

I have had one woman tell me she desired it more than her husband, and that can likely ebb and flow. But always be available to your husband and try not to tell him, "No." I have never really understood the thought process of telling my husband, "No." I was raised this way and taught my daughter the same. Maybe it is how you were raised. Maybe it has something to do with an abusive relationship in the past. If you are using sex to weaponize your relationship, then it is wrong. Using sex as a reward or punishment is wrong.

Now, are there men with unhealthy sexual needs? Yes, and in that case, you both need to be working toward healthy sexual intimacy.

Recently, I read a blog post about marriage, and although I would love for every woman to experience what I experience in my marriage, I know that is not always possible. So, I will share some of what I read:

According to Dr. Juli Slattery:

.... there are legitimate reasons why a woman might say "no" or "not now" to her husband's sexual advances. Illnesses, serious unresolved conflict, or abusive patterns are good examples. While I don't think we should automatically say yes to every invitation to have sex, I do believe we should say yes to every invitation to work on sexual intimacy.

If there is a conflict in the way of you feeling sexually safe with your husband, don't just stonewall him. Invite him to talk through the issue. Express how important it is for you to feel emotionally and sexually close. If you're exhausted, plan another time to be intimate within the next 24 hours. If you struggle with sexual pain or anxiety during sex, work together to restore healthy intimacy (Slattery, Dr. Juli).

I thought her explanations were on target. *Keep working on intimacy*. It is so important.

As far as not having sex during your period, this is a health issue. The Lord says it is, so I stand by it. Your body is cleansing itself:

> *[19] Do not approach a woman to have sexual relations during the uncleanness of her monthly period.*
> **Leviticus 18:19 (NIV)**

Hence, my rule of thumb is *let's let the body cleanse while it's cleansing*.

According to Dr. Alan Copperman (a board-certified reproductive endocrinologist and infertility specialist with a long history of success in treating infertility and applying fertility preservation technologies):

During menstrual bleeding, the cervix is normally low and hard, and slightly open to allow the blood to flow out. It feels like the tip of your nose. After your period stops, the cervix remains low and hard and the opening to the uterus remains closed (Copperman, Dr. Alan).

According to Elias E. Mazokopakis (Department of Internal Medicine, Naval Hospital of Crete, Chania, Greece; Department of Theology, National and Kapodistrian University of Athens, Athens, Greece) and George Samonis (Department of Internal Medicine, University Hospital of Heraklion, Crete, Greece) in Maedica, a Journal of Clinical Medicine, "vaginal sexual intercourse during menstruation is a possible risk factor for developing endometriosis," (Mazokopakis, Elias E. and Samonis, George).

So, it sounds like we should protect our body. God knew what He was telling us when he told us to hold off during our periods. If our husband knows the plan, and that is the only time to abstain, he will likely be okay with it.

Chapter 4 - Bible Study Questions

A) Obedience is a difficult thing for me. Well, it's difficult for any woman, after all it is our curse.

1. Do you feel you are a strong-willed woman?

2. Can you share a time when you were strong-willed?

3. Do you think that it will be difficult to control the woman inside you?

4. How can those around you help you to be a better wife? Encouragement? Advice? Counseling?

B) I wonder if you can relate to being a strong-willed woman when you read any of my stories. I shared them to tell you that my life is fulfilled in my submissiveness to God under my husband. And that all the things that my heart desires for my husband are met by being submissive to him.

1. Can you relate to the stories?

2. Do you want to be submissive to God?

3. Do you question if your heart's desires might be met in submission?

C) Sexual intimacy is important in a marriage relationship.

1. Do you struggle with being intimate with your husband?

2. If yes, how can you work toward sexual intimacy? Did any of Dr. Juli Slattery's advice help?

3. Have you ever used sex as a weapon? Like to reward or punish?

4. If yes, do you recognize this as a sin?

5. Are you ready to give this part of your life to God?

Chapter 5
Umbrella of Protection

What happens to a man when a woman respects him? Growing up in my home, my mother always showed my father respect. My dad would give her anything. Take her anywhere. They were never apart and did nothing apart from each other.

I think she could likely talk him into anything. However, a woman that shows respect to a man doesn't do that. So here is one example of that:

Recently, we booked a cruise with our four youngest children and some other friends. My parents normally go on cruises with us. I know that my mom wants to go. However, I know that something happened on the last cruise that made my dad not want to go again. I wasn't on that cruise, so I'm not sure what it was.

So, he said, "No more cruises!"

When I called my parents to see if they wanted to go on the cruise, my mom said, "Well, ask your dad."

He said, "No," and that was the end of the discussion.

Do I think that she would like to go? I know she would like to go, especially with all four of the younger grandchildren going. However, she did not try to convince him to go. There is protection in that decision for her too. When her husband says no, she is protected by his decision, and sometimes we miss that as wives. *We don't understand the protection.*

Sometimes, the Lord puts something on our husband's hearts, to make them not want to do something. We may not understand it, but it is for our protection. Now, if we are obedient to our husbands, then we stand underneath the *Umbrella of Protection*.

When you are a submissive wife, men will want to do anything for you - ANYTHING - and so it becomes difficult not using your influence to manipulate and take advantage of them. Try not to do this, as you may step out of that *Umbrella of Protection* that the Lord has given you.

According to my husband, "Men will do anything for a submissive wife because they are loving, encouraging, affirming and supportive. It brings out the best in a man. A submissive wife is such a blessing, and he wants to take his responsibility, to love her and take care of her, seriously. Men don't even think about it, it just happens as a response to the wife's submission."

This doesn't mean there are times you can't change his mind or that it's wrong to change his mind. Have you ever wondered how Sarah convinced Abraham to take Hagar and have a baby? Well, when you begin to be a submissive wife, it won't take long to understand.

> *[2] so she said to Abram, "The Lord has kept me from having children. Go, sleep with my slave; perhaps I can build a family through her." Abram agreed to what Sarai said.*
> **Genesis 16:2 (NIV)**

Let's just say the Hagar idea was a bad idea!

Going back to Sarah's story, recall the Lord had closed her womb. Therefore, she was protected from what I believe, (and what others that are more educated in Scripture than I believe), could have been a problem when she was married to the Pharaoh. However, because she desperately wanted a baby, she took things into her own hands. She was stepping outside that *Umbrella of Protection*.

Sarah caused great conflict in her family that some believe continues even today between the Jews and Palestinian Arabs. It is said that their fight for the land (Jerusalem) today stems from the two brothers, Isaac and Ishmael. The Jews are the descendants of Isaac, and the Palestinian Arabs are the descendants of Ishmael (Urban, J. Kristen).

Had Sarah waited on the Lord to provide her with the child of promise and not taken things in her own hands, especially a decision of this magnitude, then this would not have been a problem. I would like to add a caveat to this story. This was a common practice, in the land around them. However, this was not a common practice for Sarah and Abraham. They had been set apart.

What is important to understand is that Abraham had basically given up on having a child and told God, "Well, the one who will inherit my estate will be a servant in my household."

He had no intention of having any relations outside of his wife. God said no, you will have a child. Also, as we can see in the Scripture, it was credited to him as righteousness because he believed the Lord.

Then, I wonder how he let Sarah convince him to take a slave and get her pregnant, to have an heir? Was it because he loved her? Was it because she meant everything to him? Perhaps, she convinced him to do it. It wasn't because he didn't believe God!

Or that he didn't think God couldn't do amazing things. He had seen the amazing things that God had done, and he believed God. Read the Scripture and see where God tells him he will have that child:

[1] After this, the word of the Lord came to Abram in a vision: "Do not be afraid, Abram. I am your shield, your very great reward." [2] But Abram said, "Sovereign Lord, what can you give me since I remain childless and the one who will inherit my estate is Eliezer of Damascus?" [3] And Abram said, "You have given me no children; so a servant in my household will be my heir." [4] Then the word of the Lord came to him: "This man will not be your heir, but a son who is your own flesh and blood will be your heir." [5] He took him outside and said, "Look up at the sky and count the stars--if indeed you can count them." Then he said to him, "So shall your offspring be." [6] Abram believed the Lord, and he credited it to him as righteousness.
Genesis 15:1-6 (NIV)

As years pass by, Sarah becomes disheartened and says, "The Lord hasn't let me have children, so take my slave and have a baby, and we can have children through her," (Paraphrased, Gen. 16:2).

Even though this was a common practice for the world at that time, why give up on God now? The fact that they had finally given up on God and felt they needed to help Him out was a mistake:

[1] Now Sarai, Abram's wife, had borne him no children. But she had an Egyptian slave named Hagar; [2] so she said to Abram, "The Lord has kept me from having children. Go, sleep with my slave; perhaps I can build a family through her." Abram agreed to what Sarai said. [3] So after Abram had been living in Canaan ten years, Sarai his wife took her Egyptian slave Hagar and gave her to her husband to be his wife. [4] He slept with Hagar, and she conceived. When she knew she was pregnant, she began to despise her mistress. [5] Then Sarai said to Abram, "You are responsible for the wrong I am suffering. I put my slave in your arms, and now that she knows she is pregnant, she despises me. May the Lord judge between you and me." [6] "Your slave is in your hands," Abram said. "Do with her whatever you think best." Then Sarai mistreated Hagar; so she fled from her.
Genesis 16:1-6 (NIV)

Sarah regretted her decision and then blamed her husband because he didn't tell her it was a bad idea and put his foot down. Too bad! This is a great lesson for us to learn from in the end.

Sometimes, as Christians, we might get lost in common practices and thoughts. We might forget to set ourselves apart from the things the world is doing and saying. What does this look like? Well, right now, the common practice is for a woman to be in control. We can start there! Emasculating a man is a common practice. Even thought of as being comical. I, however, find nothing funny about it!

I have a hard time turning on the T.V. and finding any shows lifting a man up. Instead, most are tearing men down in marriages. They are presenting them as a stupid partner and the woman as the intelligent partner who has all the common sense. No wonder the women I talk to think that men have no common sense. *We are being brainwashed!*

Eve is another example of not following God or her husband but drawing her husband into eating the fruit and stepping outside the *Umbrella of Protection*. Eve caused a curse on women and all of humanity.

I cannot name all of the times that my husband has told me, "No!" They are too numerous in the past twenty years. However, I know that in all those times, I know that my obedience protected me! I may never know how, and that is okay. I don't need to know. He is here to protect me as a *weaker vessel*, and I need to take my position as the weaker vessel. Notice God's warning to our husbands:

[7] Husbands, in the same way be considerate as you live with your wives, and treat them with respect as the weaker partner and as heirs with you of the gracious gift of life, so that nothing will hinder your prayers.
1 Peter 3:7 (NIV)

I don't share this with you to hold it over your husband's head but to show you the Lord loves you and has a design for you - to be cared for deeply. He can get ahold of your husband for you!

He flat-out told them, "I won't even listen to your prayers!" Woah!

When I began respecting my husband, I didn't expect the blessings that would follow. The blessings of my children and how they act (my husband's actions play a huge role in this, too) and how my husband views me and loves me is priceless. It builds the mortar in our "brick wall of strength" if I had to portray our marriage, in some way.

When a woman respects a man. A man would die for her. He would do anything for her. She becomes priceless to him. I don't have a fear of him wandering. Not that these aren't things he couldn't do, but I think he would be crazy if he did. So it gives freedom to the wife. *He wants to cherish the beauty encouraging him and lifting him up.*

One night, as I was sitting with some unsaved friends, playing a game, I could see it.

I was semi-jokingly saying, "Of course, I have to be obedient to my husband."

Not that I was joking about being obedient to my husband. It was the timing of the comment in the situation.

But the reason I mention this situation is that my friend's boyfriend's eyes lit up, and he started saying, "Yes, listen to her."

However, my friend was oblivious to what was going on because we were all laughing, and the laughing was drowning out all the comments. I was well aware of what he was craving and asking for. Men want their significant others to show them respect. A man needs respect like a woman needs love.

Chapter 5 - Bible Study Questions

A) Sometimes, the Lord puts something on our husbands' hearts, to make them not want to do something. We may not understand it, but it is for our protection. And if we are obedient to them, then we stand underneath the *Umbrella of Protection.*

1. Have you ever been told "no" by your spouse?

2. Did you talk him into changing his mind?

3. How did the situation work out?

4. Have you ever thought about the protection that is provided for you by your husband's decisions?

B) The real problem comes when you are a submissive wife. These men want to do anything for you, ANYTHING, and so it becomes difficult not using that influence to get your way and take advantage of them. Try not to do this, as you may step out of that umbrella that the Lord has given you.

1. Have you ever thought about how amazing it is to have a husband that would do just about anything for you?

2. Does this give you the desire to be a submissive wife?

3. Do you see how Sarah convinced Abraham to take Hagar as a wife?

C) When a woman respects a man. A man would die for her. He would do anything for her. She becomes priceless to him.

1. How much do these statements mean to you?

2. Can you see them in your life now?

3. If no? Will you be trying to respect your husband so you can see the rewards?

D) A man needs respect like a woman needs love. Often, women don't know what respect is.

1. Do you know what respect is?

2. Do you sometimes think that respect is love?

3. Are you understanding that respect is obedience?

4. How hard is it or will it be for you to respect your husband?

Chapter 6
Discord in Discipline

It's hard for a mother when a father is disciplining a child. We, as mothers, want to step in and rescue that child. In my first marriage, I did that all too often.

I remember my middle child getting a good spanking. It was right before my divorce, and I crawled in bed with him and told him he didn't have to worry because those spankings would not happen like that anymore. I thought I was rescuing him.

It's funny because years later when he became a teenager, he decided he wanted to go live with his dad. That decision actually really hurt my feelings. I remember thinking how hard I had worked to protect him and *how could he possibly want to go back to that lifestyle?*

It's interesting to think that boys want and need that father figure in their life. No matter how hard the father is on them. I would add, not just the father figure, as they had the father figure with my second husband, but they wanted their father, at whatever cost. At least, I thought it was at whatever cost.

I felt they were giving up so much, leaving all of their brothers, sister and mom to go live with a dad who was a tough dad. Not like their kind-hearted stepdad. However, I was reminded by my husband that when children are only around their parents for short amounts of time, they become *"Disney World"* parents. Everything is fun in those short times they are with them.

I had never lost custody of my children but made a decision it was in their best interest to live with their dad. Also, possibly in my best interest, not to go to court and lose custody, so I could still bring them home, if I needed to, which happened several years later.

DISCIPLINE

I wasn't much into spanking. My rule of thumb for my daughter was if *you hit me...I spank you.* Other than that, no spankings for her. So, she knew if she hit me she would get a spanking. She didn't hit me too much. I didn't like spanking girls because.... I didn't like to get spanked myself. Therefore, in my mind, I equated that to be *you shouldn't spank girls.*

As a young girl, I had a soft heart, and my parents could talk to me, and I wanted to do what was right. Spanking me made me mad. So, why spank me? I can tell you, I didn't want to make my daughter mad!

But I didn't realize there was a difference between boys and girls. Another reason I didn't like to spank was that I didn't want to spank them out of anger, and when I was younger, they seemed to make me angry a lot.

So, when my husband would spank them, I would run to their rescue and undermine him. Or, if he gave them a strong, stern talking to, I would sweetly say, "You understand don't you?" to try to soften his tone. *I didn't realize I was not helping my boys become men, at all.*

I don't think women have a clue what boys need when being raised, but men do! Believe it or not, that is what they are giving them, and all too often, we are in the way!

When I got married the second time, and the Lord got ahold of me, my husband and I had four more children. So I had seven in the house. We had six boys and one girl. He taught me that boys need a stern talking to and sometimes a spanking. Thus, I got out of his way.

When we began to homeschool our children out of necessity, I would say, "Okay, well, when Dad gets home, I will let him deal with you."

Then, when he would walk in the door, I would say, "Can you deal with this one and that one?"

He would say, "Yes, I can!"

He was the enforcer. He never even asked me the crime. He was only there to enforce the punishment. Not out of anger but out of need. We became a team!

When my husband and I parented together, I would not say we were on the same page. He thought I should spank my daughter. I didn't think she should ever get a spanking. The same was true for the boys for me. I was inserting how I felt I should have been raised through my children. I think that is often how people raise their children. We raise them how we wanted to be raised, not how we were raised.

When I got married, my husband explained that my boys needed to be toughened up and be prepared to be men and that I would not understand that. Not to say he would have to spank them. However, they did not always need to be spoken to with a soft voice or sweet tone, but maybe more of a military tone or a harsh voice. Also, we might expect a "Yes, Sir" to follow. Showing respect or that they understood he was in charge.

He explained if they were not raised this way, they would not be prepared for the real world. When tough things came their way, they would crumble. I was surprised, but now understood why I had been raised the way I had been raised. I was not raised to be soft or to crumble, but I was a girl. There is still a balance there. I think you can raise a daughter, understanding the necessity to be strong, without the need to beat it into her, *per se*.

According to my husband, "I don't think that the woman should intervene during the act of discipline unless there is obvious danger to the child. If there are concerns, she should talk to him about her concerns later, in private. Otherwise, the wife disrespects the husband, and the children disrespect the father, as well. It undermines the discipline and is confusing for the child."

Children today are too soft. This might be because they are raised by women, and we are soft. I would not have understood the difference had my husband not taught me. Let your husband be harder on your boys to make them men. Also, maybe help him see that girls need to be dealt with gently. Be a team together.

I see a correlation between the harder I was raised, the more I didn't think I needed a man telling me what to do. I was a fighter. Hence, raising a daughter gently can help her be gentle and more submissive in her role. At least, maybe not a fighter at every turn.

PARENTING

The biggest thing I can tell you is the more children I have, the less I feel I know. I find that people that have an only child tend to think they have the parenting cornered. I have listened to them give me advice, and all the while, I was thinking, *do you know how many children I have? And you have one?* Just because it worked with your one child doesn't mean it will work with mine. This is true in my life.

I have one daughter and give advice about how to raise daughters. However, as parents, we can trust in the Lord and His promises and truths. I can hold firm to the promises of God.

[6] Start children off on the way they should go, and even when they are old they will not turn from it.
Proverbs 22:6 (NIV)

As I said before, one thing I am not big on is spankings. But I'm a girl. Now, if a boy were reading this, maybe he would say, *what does that have to do with anything?* Then again, maybe a girl would, too. Everyone is different; we are all made differently. I thank the Lord we are made differently.

As I present this, I have to look at each child differently. Additionally, each child needs something different. Parenting is not too difficult, but it is not a cookie-cutter, one size fits all, either. Therefore, paying attention to your children is important. *If you're making them angry, then maybe you need to stop whatever you are doing and listen.*

[21] Fathers, do not embitter your children, or they will become discouraged.
Colossians 3:21 (NIV)

[4] Fathers, do not exasperate your children; instead, bring them up in the training and instruction of the Lord.
Ephesians 6:4 (NIV)

Don't think that only fathers can exasperate or embitter your children. Be in prayer for your children and try to train, encourage, love, and listen to them, with the necessity of discipline.

Chapter 6 - Bible Study Questions

A) Do you find yourself stepping in between your husband and your child when he or she is being disciplined?

1. What are ways you can stop this from happening?

2. Do you see that there is a need for children, especially boys, to be disciplined by the father?

3. How can you get on the same page with your husband, so you don't have issues when time comes for them to be disciplined?

B) *"[4] Fathers, do not exasperate your children; instead, bring them up in the training and instruction of the Lord."* Ephesians 6:4 (NIV).

1. What does this Scripture mean to you?

2. How often do you talk to your children?

3. How can you and your husband talk about this Scripture and get on the same page?

4. Do you see the importance of letting your husband deal with the children and not coming between them?

C) My husband had to teach me what my boys needed discipline-wise. And I had to help my husband understand what my daughter needed.

1. How can you sit down and come up with a plan to know what you both will do?

2. Are you open to listening to your husband and what he feels the children need when raising them?

3. How can you show respect for your husband's decisions in raising the children?

4. Do you understand that your children will reflect with bad behavior in response to you undermining your husband?

Chapter 7
The Woman's Role

UNDERSTANDING THE WOMAN'S ROLE

So often, I hear the words… "I don't feel like my husband is doing his part spiritually or he's not leading us like he should be. So now I have to do it!"

If a woman would take her position, then a man would take his.

Sometimes, as women, we feel we are supposed to do things to become more spiritual and be more godly, and it's really never enough. Most husbands do not feel called to go on these "get holier than everybody in church" adventures with us. Like mission trips, women's conferences, Bible studies, couples conferences, etc.

Now, I'm not knocking it. Would the Lord have been able to teach this had I not been trying to cover my head and start that new Bible study?

I heard a woman say one time, "The Lord is calling me to go on a mission trip," but her husband was not on board.

What she was alluding to was that her husband wasn't listening to the Lord. I was friends with her, and we talked about how the husband is the head of the home. How the Lord could not call her to go without calling him, as he is the husband. Also, if her husband told her no, then that was absolute. Then it could not have come from the Lord.

See, if the husband is the head of the household, then the Lord is not going to tell a woman and not the man about the mission trip. So often as women, we become so spiritual, but we forget that our spiritual job is to be submissive to our husbands.

Well, let's be honest; some of us just don't know anything about this. Again, we see ourselves as equal to our husbands under God. We have heard about submission but don't know much more about it except it's demeaning, and I want nothing to do with it. However, if I could share how freeing it is and how wonderful it is. How the curse has fed us a lie, and we could have men loving us to the nth degree, then we would be all in! But instead, we are defeated.

We get so spiritual that our husbands step in the shadows and can't lead. We set a standard that our husbands think they can't live up to, so they quit. As the more spiritual the husband becomes (let's be honest), the woman gets even more spiritual, as they are going to out-trump them. So why try? It's like a placement that the husband can't achieve.

If the woman would take her place and be submissive and try to learn from her husband, then he would have the desire to try to teach her and lead her. This is what was trying to be taught in 1 Timothy 2:11-12:

[11] A woman should learn in quietness and full submission. [12] I do not permit a woman to teach or to assume authority over a man; she must be quiet. ...
1 Timothy 2:11-12 (NIV)

Some people think this is in reference to the church. This is also talking about a husband and wife. Not that this has no reference to the church. I have no authority in that regard. Thank goodness!

I certainly have to have the Lord help me with this Scripture and be open and in submission to it. I try to remember to live in grace, love and truth. Blessings come from my obedience.

Most women think that their husbands know little about a spiritual walk. I think they would be surprised if they sat down and talked to their husband and asked questions and listened. If you want your husband to grow, the best way would be for you to encourage him, build him up and have him teach you. But either way, a woman is to take her place.

I was pleasantly surprised by my husband's knowledge of the Bible. He knew so much. His knowledge was so grand. But nobody would know it because he's so quiet. I didn't find out what my husband knew until I asked him questions. And boy, what a surprise it was. So, I want to encourage you to ask questions. In addition, if he doesn't know, he will learn from trying to teach you!

Now, what would it hurt to at least just try this for, say, five months? You will see immediate results. I'm not saying it will become second nature as you must grow spiritually with the process and be obedient to the Lord. Furthermore, the decision will ultimately be to do this for the Lord and not your husband. But to try something to see the blessings is so worth it.

So what does this look like, you may ask? Often when I go to church, I have many questions regarding the service. I come home, and I will ask my husband questions. I did this early in our marriage to make sure that we were one in our thoughts and how we viewed Scripture.

Now if you wonder what happens if you disagree... well, that could happen. Additionally, it could happen often if you don't take your role as a submissive wife. So let me help you to combat the disagreements. It is not your role to teach your husband first off. It is the Holy Spirit's role. So sit back and let him take the reins. You are allowing him to lead. *You are giving the incentive for your husband to want to teach you.*

So let's say you have a question for your husband regarding the service. Let's also say you do not agree with his answer. Your next job is to find the supportive Scripture in the Bible you need for him to help to clarify. This Scripture would be in direct conflict with what you feel he is teaching.

So you would simply say to him, *"Could you explain this Scripture to me?"*

Your job, then, is not to correct him but to listen and learn. And in the end, to get on the same page with him. Find out how he got what he got from the Scripture.

Additionally, if you thought something different, you might say, "*I always thought this meant this....*" He and you can become a great team together doing this.

If you feel he is still wrong, then pray for the Holy Spirit to teach him. He will teach him.

I remember when I turned to a friend who I was co-teaching a Bible study with about grace. We were having a discussion on the passage in Romans 7 about grace and we didn't agree. I was done arguing!

Then, I told him, "I will pray that the Holy Spirit reveals this to you." I will share more about this story in a later chapter.

Well, he did! God revealed we were both wrong about grace. He can teach your husband, too. In His time. In His way. Also, maybe He needs to teach you. As I was wrong. It would not be a good idea to say, "I will pray for the Holy Spirit to teach this to you" to your husband! Secretly pray to the Holy Spirit! As again, I was not correct, and you do not want to burn a bridge, but come together with him.

What I found is how much my husband and I were on the same page about everything. I know this is not always common, but we both listened to each other and learned from each other. A husband needs respect, and respecting his responses can build him up, and build his love for you! I know that if I ever tried to force-feed him in God's word, I'm not sure he would have been receptive as I am not the Holy Spirit and not his teacher. I must keep that in perspective.

Some of the other ways I got my husband to teach me was by doing a Bible study on my own, and when I learned something or disagreed with something, I came to him.

Recently I attended a Bible study at church, and the Bible study was on women of the Bible. When it spoke about Sarah, it talked about how Sarah should have told her husband "no," regarding the fact that she would tell people she was his sister and therefore not have done the very things she was commended for.

Okay, wait. This is my passion! How could someone contradict the Bible in a Bible study?

I was shocked. I asked my husband about it. He agreed with me. We then made an appointment to meet with the woman and her husband who was leading the Bible study to discuss what her views were on Sarah. I didn't want to show up at a Bible study and blindside someone with my views. I wanted to be submissive and quiet (which is not at all my personality) but to bring to light what I thought was a flaw.

So to do this, I put this in my husband's lap as I knew he would handle it with love and tenderness. The woman and her husband agreed with us, and we left knowing I wouldn't have to worry about it. I felt I could come to the study and be quiet. Which again, is not my personality, but it was my mission as she knew where I stood, and I wanted to honor her role in however she wanted to progress in the study.

I think as you grow daily that your husband can rejoice with you as you are learning, *even in this book*. Discussing it with him will help him be able to lead you. You will learn more about him if you ask him questions about what I am saying in this book. Like how does this make him feel?

Chapter 7 - Bible Study Questions

A) We get so spiritual that our husbands step in the shadows and can't lead. The more spiritual they become, the woman gets even more spiritual as they are going to out-trump them. So why try? It's like a placement that can't be achieved.

1. Do you struggle with thinking your husband is not godly enough?

2. If yes? Do you see how you can combat this by fulfilling your role?

3. Can you think of a time you thought you were more spiritual than your husband?

4. If yes? Are you willing to put yourself in your position under your husband?

B) A husband needs respect, and respecting his responses can build him up and build his love for you!

1. If you asked him questions regarding Scripture, can you respect his responses?

2. Do you understand how not respecting his responses would be detrimental to bringing the two of you closer together toward the Lord?

3. What are some of the ways of showing respect that are talked about in the chapter?

C) If I ever came to my husband and tried to force-feed him in God's Word, I'm not sure he would have been receptive, as I am not the Holy Spirit and not his teacher. I must keep that in perspective.

1. What are ways you could approach your husband to ask him to help you learn?

2. What do you think it means by force-feeding God's word in this statement?

3. How hard will it be for you to let your husband be the teacher?

4. What ideas were presented to help you get on the same page with your husband?

D) I think, as you grow daily, that your husband can rejoice with you as you are learning, even in this book. Discussing it with him will help him be able to lead you. You will learn more about him if you ask him questions about what I am saying in this book. Like how does this make him feel?

1. How does your husband feel about this book?

2. What are some steps you are making to grow daily with your husband?

3. Do you want to discuss this book with your husband?

Chapter 8
Expectations

Be careful not to have silent expectations. And what I mean by that is that you have to share whatever expectations you may have with your husband.

Years ago, when I got married, I had and still have tendencies of an OCD person. I didn't know that I had those tendencies, but it showed when I expected my house to be cleaned all the time. And I expected him to help me with the house. Honestly, I had been raised this way, so I thought this was the way everyone was. I remember one time my ex telling me it's okay to sit down. But in my mind, I didn't have time to do that and get everything done.

I went to marriage counseling alone one time, and the marriage counselor caught wind of what I was doing.

He said, "OK, listen, I'm going to allow you to clean one room a day."

I looked at him and thought, *"How can I do that?"* I was cleaning every room every day and making everybody miserable doing it. I like having a clean house, and I like having an organized house. So when my house gets out of control, I feel like I'm out of control. If it gets too out of control, it might stay out of control because I won't know where to fix the problem.

So I told him I would try to do it, and I began to only clean one room a day. And so began my learning that it was not normal to clean every room every day.

I don't think that my parents cleaned every room every day as I did, but every room was in order.

I took it one step further. So working a full-time job and then coming home and taking care of my three children, I would have a full house to clean sometimes until four in the morning before I had to go to work the next day.

My true learning from this marriage counselor was that I needed to talk to my spouse and explain what was going on instead of getting upset. My expectations were unreasonable, but I had no idea. He did. And he was trying to tell me. By telling me it was okay to sit down.

I think that I had a clue one time when I moved to live closer to my parents, and I walked by my son's room, and I could hear my oldest son say to my middle son, "No, Mom wants them to be in alphabetical order." He was referring to the videos we owned when they were putting them up. He was only ten, and I felt bad he felt pressure to be perfect in putting them away.

Now if we don't tell our spouses what we expect from them, then we get angry with them for not fulfilling our expectations, and they have no idea what we are upset about.

Often I feel we all have things that we desire, whether it is to have a perfectly clean home, an organized bookshelf, a clean desk, a perfectly kept lawn, or whatever, but putting it on the spouse sometimes can be unreasonable. I recognize it now, at least. And I live my life knowing I could be single as I was. So, I live doing things expecting nothing from my spouse.

That may be hard to believe, but I don't expect him to do anything. He goes to work, and that is great. I'll take the trash out, clean the house, shovel the driveway, mow the lawn, anything I can do if I can get away with it. I do this out of love for him. I want to alleviate his burden, so he can relax when he comes home from work. Most of the time, he insists on helping me with the chores.

I am not a cook, but I will try to make things on occasion. But my husband loves to cook. He is the "chef of all chefs." So if he weren't, I would likely try to cook more. He does, on occasion, call me and tell me to put something on the stove or in the oven. Personally, I don't even think about food.

I remember before getting married again, my kids asking, "What are we going to eat?"

I simply replied, "I don't know; what are you going to make?" So, they were excited that I married someone who likes to cook.

Recently, my husband and I went outside to move cars from our driveway after it had snowed. The plow was coming to clear the driveway. I wanted to shovel the snow before my husband drove the car on the snow. But he was frustrated (after all, he pays to have someone plow the driveway. And we were moving the cars for the plows).

The problem is when he drives on the snow it smashes the snow into the driveway, and you can't get it up. So, I asked if I could shovel it before he backed up. He was a little annoyed with me because I didn't listen. I started shoveling without him and hurt my back. I felt bad because he shoveled, too. But I told him he didn't have to.

I said, "I just wanted to shovel before he drove on the snow." We talked about it later.

I said, "I just want our driveway to look like the ones across the street that are so nice and clean and have no ice on them, and if I shovel before you drive on them, I won't have to spend hours later getting the ice off."

He said, "I understand, but we aren't like the people across the street. They are old and don't take their cars out of the garage. So that is not our life right now."

I will not say that my idea of having a clean driveway will change. It is a desire of my heart. It is an OCD issue. Like my home. But I have heard him, and he is correct. So I need to listen to him and not make his life miserable just because I like a clean driveway!

When we recently moved, we were having our furniture delivered to our new home, and I was so happy to have no furniture and so stressed to think about having a ton of furniture come.

I told my husband, "Don't be surprised if I tell the movers to keep driving."

But the day arrived, and when they showed up, I was able to accept the furniture and not wave them on. They were delivering twice as much furniture as my house would hold. I was proud of myself for not waving them on. Every day is a process for me to work through having to have things so-so. I feel like if I can do it, anybody can do it.

There are a few things in the house that my husband and I have talked about. We have an understanding that I cannot handle any part of the house if it is left unkempt. Specifically, a messy kitchen. So, he helps me the best he can. But I also know that this is my issue and not his, so I work hard to carry that burden alone and appreciate whatever help he gives me.

Now if the situation is in reverse and the husband requires attention to the house. I would recommend getting rid of as much clutter as you can and limiting the mess that will be around.

My poor children tell me stories now that they are adults of how I used to tell them to pick three toys. And how my middle son loved all of his toys. As for the rest of his toys, I would get rid of them. I just couldn't stand the clutter. However, picking three toys was so terrible for him because he loved all of his toys.

I don't think my actions were correct in how I tried to solve my problem of keeping my house clean. One of my kids told me they now let their kids pick a certain amount of toys and then put the others up in storage for a short time. Later they bring those toys out and put the toys they were playing with up. It's like having new toys. That sounds much nicer and less traumatizing. Maybe I needed their counsel back then.

We don't want to assume our husband knows what we are thinking. They probably don't. After working hard and having a stressful day, many times they don't want to come home and think at all. Which is interesting. As I don't think, as women, we can turn our brains off.

I don't think, as women, we understand much about men. According to my husband, men honestly can sit and think of nothing. How can a man sit for a while and think about nothing? In about two minutes, I've thought about fifty things.

Additionally, men have a hard time expressing their feelings. Women need to express their feelings. According to an article published by MSU, "men often express feelings outwardly through body language, such as physical gestures, facial changes, muscle tensing and gritting teeth, instead of expressing those emotions with words." (Zoromski, Kevin).

We have been made differently. So, if you have a need or desire, share that with your husband. Do not assume he knows what you are thinking, needing, or wanting. Find ways to talk to him. Let him know what your needs are and what you expect from him. And, whether it is to calm him down or lift him up, be a help mate with your words.

Chapter 8 - Bible Study Questions

A) Be careful not to have silent expectations. And what I mean by that is that you have to share whatever expectations you may have with your husband.

1. What are expectations you have in the home?

2. Are there any expectations you haven't shared with your husband you expect him to do or keep up with? Like taking out the trash.

3. How upset do you get when your expectations are not met?

4. What are ways you can help your husband meet your expectations?

B) We don't want to assume our husband knows what we are thinking.

1. Do you assume most of the time that your husband knows what you want?

2. What are expectations that we have that you might assume he knows?

3. How can you stop assuming he knows what you want and remember to tell him?

C) Women and men are different.

1. How are men and women different?

2. How can we help men to understand what we need from them?

3. Are you one that tends to share your expectations earlier or after you are angry? Or do you find yourself thinking your husband automatically knows?

Chapter 9
Build Your Husband Up

IF YOU WANT AN AMAZING HUSBAND, BUILD HIM UP

I don't think women realize how they play a role in the development of their husband. We need to build him up and not tear him down.

I heard recently that society thinks that men are stupid. That is crazy.

I have six boys, and not one of them is stupid. They are all very intelligent. They are brilliant. However, I have seen them date women who can tear them down, and I have seen them date women who can build them up.

Unfortunately, they sometimes don't see that they are being torn down. Instead, they feel defeated by their failures.

When one of my boys was in high school, he was dating a girl that was a year older than him. So when she graduated and went to college, she got a job waiting tables and made good money. However, he was still in high school, working a part-time job and making minimum wage. I could tell he was feeling defeated at some point, but I didn't know why.

Later that year, I received a phone call from his boss asking me if I knew about his relationship and how his girlfriend was putting him down because he wasn't making as much money as she was. I was shocked, and irritated. But we had to be careful because we couldn't approach him about what we knew when we weren't supposed to know it. Plus, we couldn't give away our source.

I tried to dance around the subject with him by talking about how important it is to be respected by your wife or girlfriend. It was very concerning to me because they were just dating, and if he is already feeling like a failure and he is in high school, how will this play out later?

He was talking about asking her to marry him. I did not think that was a good idea. He needed to be built up and not torn down. How can she tell him he is not good enough when he is in high school working a part-time job? He didn't even need the money, and really he was working for our friends to have a job and be busy. He was also learning responsibility and hard work.

This was not a good relationship. It scared me. When I talked to him about the subject, he would make excuses for how I didn't know the relationship and his faults and how he needed to be better. So, he was being torn down.

Even if a man is not doing well in one area of his life, if he is encouraged in the other areas of his life, then he will improve in the area he is not doing well.

However, if he is continuously torn down, then he might get frustrated easily, as I see in some of my children today. They get into video games, maybe to numb the pain. Other guys may turn to drinking or other things to numb the pain. But it is easy to build a man up. To encourage him. Find things to tell him he does well. We need to remember we are not the Holy Spirit. We need to pray and ask the Holy Spirit to convict the hearts of our husbands. And not try to be the Holy Spirit.

Often I have women tell me that their husband sits at home and won't find a job. You could help him find that job, sending out resumes and setting up job interviews. You could be the secretary. I think that often men find difficulty in looking for a job. And even if they don't find it difficult to look for a job, helping them find a job can help them find an even better job than if they were looking by themselves.

Instead of bashing the husband for not finding a job, be a team member with your husband. You are his helper.

> **And the LORD God said, "It is not good that man should be alone; I will make him a helper comparable to him."**
> **Genesis 2:18-25 (NKJV)**

One way I support my husband is by always helping him with his jobs. I help my husband find every job he gets. I make my husband's resume. When we go to the conferences where the job scouts are, I am the go-between. When they ask to speak to him, I tell them I will present the job, and we will see what he says. I walk around to every job booth and talk to everyone.

Then I present the jobs to my husband and let him decide which job is worth his time. I am his partner, his secretary, his greatest supporter. I take the greatest pride in helping him with his jobs. I know that his time is precious, and I know he doesn't want to do it. So I don't make him do it. Plus, why would I want to see him fail at it. He is so successful with his jobs because, as a team, we work together.

You can present other ways of being your husband's helper. For example, doing his laundry so he has less to think about, taking care of finances and budget, cooking food from home to save money, not being a burden by spending money on unnecessary things, etc. Ask him what things you can take on to help him more. This is how you can be a helper to him.

You can make or break your husband.

[1] The wise woman builds her house, but with her own hands the foolish one tears hers down.
Proverbs 14:1 (NIV)

I feel the Geneva College best summed up this Scripture with this statement:

How does a foolish woman pull down her own house? By carelessly or spitefully adopting destructive habits that alienate and impoverish her family. She commits adultery with another man -- or woman. She spends money the family does not have or invests the family fortune foolishly in what she does not understand. She mocks, undercuts, and derides her man, robbing him of confidence and courage. She demands her own way, even with tears and threats, until she gets what she wants. She whispers to her children she, not their father, really loves them, while she subtly, or not so subtly, undercuts his authority (Edgar, Dr. Bill).

[19] Better to live in a desert than with a quarrelsome and nagging wife.
Proverbs 21:19 (NIV)

[24] Better to live on a corner of the roof than share a house with a quarrelsome wife.
Proverbs 25:24 (NIV)

[15] A quarrelsome wife is like the dripping of a leaky roof in a rainstorm; [16] restraining her is like restraining the wind or grasping oil with the hand.
Proverbs 27:15-16 (NIV)

Solomon loved being married, but he could tell you here. Don't do it. If she is going to argue with you, then just stay single. It's not worth it.

Is that the wife you want to be? Sometimes we learn from our parents how to act. We may have picked up some behaviors from watching them. Know that we need to learn from the Spirit today how to interact with our spouse.

Your husband needs you. He wants your support. I want to encourage you to build your husband up. Know that you have a great influence on him and on the outcome of the person he will become. Help him to be successful, and rejoice with him when he succeeds. So try to build him up and make him that *Ultimate Husband* you want and need!

Chapter 9 - Bible Study Questions

A) Women don't realize that they are responsible for the *Ultimate Husband*. We need to build him up and not tear him down.

1. What are ways a wife tears down a husband?

2. Do you think a wife knows she is affecting the husband by her words?

3. What are things that you know you need to stop saying to your husband?

4. What are areas of his life he is good at doing?

5. How can you show him support in those areas?

B) Unfortunately, men sometimes don't see that they are being torn down and instead feel responsible for the failures. Even if the failures aren't their failures to be responsible for.

Example: They aren't making as much money as the wife.

1. Can you think of other examples?

2. How can you prevent this from happening?

3. Can you recall a time in your husband's life or a friend's life when you saw this happen?

4. What are positive things we can praise him for and focus on?

C) Even if a man is not doing well in one area of his life, if he is encouraged in the other areas of his life, then he will improve in the area he is not doing well.

1. Can you think of something or things that your husband is good at doing?

2. Write down ways you can encourage him in those areas.

3. Have you ever brought up an area where he is struggling?

4. If yes, pray and ask the Lord to help you to give these areas to Him and to help you focus on his good qualities.

D) We need to remember we are not the Holy Spirit. We need to pray and ask the Holy Spirit to convict the hearts of our husbands, and not try to be the Holy Spirit.

1. When would be the easiest time for you to pray, morning or evening?

2. How can you find time to be fervent in prayer for your husband and his success?

3. Prayerfully ask the Lord to help you not to be your husband's Holy Spirit.

E) I take the greatest pride in helping my husband with finding his jobs. I know that his time is precious, and I know he doesn't want to do it. So I don't expect him to do it. Plus, why would I want to see him fail at it. He is so successful with his jobs because as a team we work together.

1. What does your husband not like to do?

2. How can you help your husband?

3. Do you find you have expectations for him?

4. Does he know what those expectations are?

5. Do these expectations cause problems in the marriage?

6. If yes, then should you not have that expectation of him (Example: I mow the lawn myself)?

F) Sometimes we learn from our parents how to act. We may have picked up some behaviors from watching them.

1. What do you see yourself doing in your marriage that your mother does or did?

2. Is there something you think needs to change?

Chapter 10
Free to Obey

I remember while growing up, I was brought up under the law. I was taught to live by the law. What I mean by that is that when I sinned, I was told to ask for forgiveness and basically not taught that I was already forgiven for the sin before committing the sin.

So when I sinned, I always sought forgiveness for the sin, not realizing as a Christian that the sin was forgiven already at the cross. That we are called to confess our sins and to acknowledge our sins before the Lord. To agree with the Holy Spirit that what we did was a sin. So often when I do something wrong, the Holy Spirit says that wasn't right. And what I say is, "I know, I'm sorry." Now, I agree with the Holy Spirit, which is what I am called to do. I'm not sure if I was taught God's grace or I just didn't understand it.

Years later, I was co-teaching a Bible study with a friend on Romans. When we got to Romans 7, neither of us could understand it nor explain it. I mean, Paul was talking gibberish. What did he mean by everything he wanted to do he didn't do and everything he didn't want to do he was doing…. And who would save this wretched man…? (Paraphrased, Romans 7:19, 20, 24).

[15] I do not understand what I do. For what I want to do I do not do, but what I hate I do. [16] And if I do what I do not want to do, I agree that the law is good. [17] As it is, it is no longer I myself who do it, but it is sin living in me. [18] For I know that good itself does not dwell in me, that is, in my sinful nature. For I have the desire to do what is good, but I cannot carry it out. [19] For I do not do the good I want to do, but the evil I do not want to do---this I keep on doing. [20] Now if I do what I do not want to do, it is no longer I who do it, but it is sin living in me that does it.
Romans 7:15-20 (NIV)

[24] What a wretched man I am! Who will rescue me from this body that is subject to death? [25] Thanks be to God, who delivers me through Jesus Christ our Lord! So then, I myself in my mind am a slave to God's law, but in my sinful nature a slave to the law of sin.
Romans 7:24-25 (NIV)

We both had an opinion about what Paul was talking about. But in the end, we dismissed our Bible study.

We continued our argument all the way to our cars, and I said to him as he continued to try to explain his side, "I pray the Lord reveals this to you (as if I knew)."

Now I don't remember what I thought I knew. I didn't think I knew exactly what it was saying I knew what he was saying was not right. So that is why I said *I pray the Lord reveals this to you.* So I was sure he was way off- which he was, and I was- but the Spirit was about to wake us both up.

Anyway, the next day, he called me in tears, telling me that the Lord had revealed to him the Scripture and what it meant. He explained about God's grace and that Paul was trying to explain God's grace. He showed me.

[1] Therefore, there is now no condemnation for those who are in Christ Jesus, [2] because through Christ Jesus the law of the Spirit who gives life has set you free from the law of sin and death. **Romans 8:1-2 (NIV)**

He then showed me…

[21] I do not set aside the grace of God, for if righteousness could be gained through the law, Christ died for nothing! **Galatians 2:21 (NIV)**

I was thinking Paul was crazy!

I had always lived under the law. I couldn't believe there was such a thing as living under grace.

I needed to find where Jesus said this. So off I went in search of Jesus' teaching of grace. Specifically, grace. Only to find that this is the very thing that Christ was trying to teach when he said…

[37] Jesus replied: "'Love the Lord your God with all your heart and with all your soul and with all your mind.' [38] This is the first and greatest commandment. [39] And the second is like it: 'Love your neighbor as yourself.'" **Matthew 22:37-39 (NIV)**

He wasn't saying do this and do that. He was saying love others. It was a change of heart. If you would love others and love God, then you wouldn't break the commands out of love. And Paul said the very commands made me want to break them. He tries to explain them.

In John 4:21, Jesus tries to explain this very thought process to a Samaritan woman. He says a time will come when true worshipers will worship the Father in Spirit and in truth, for they are the kind of worshipers the Father seeks…. his worshipers **must** worship in spirit and truth.

> *[21] "Woman," Jesus replied, "believe me, a time is coming when you will worship the Father neither on this mountain nor in Jerusalem. [22] You Samaritans worship what you do not know; we worship what we do know, for salvation is from the Jews. [23] Yet a time is coming and has now come when the true worshipers will worship the Father in the Spirit and in truth, for they are the kind of worshipers the Father seeks. [24] God is spirit, and his worshipers must worship in the Spirit and in truth."*
> **John 4:21-24 (NIV)**

According to Gotquestions.org:

Grace is a constant theme in the Bible, and it culminates in the New Testament with the coming of Jesus (John 1:17). The word translated "grace" in the New Testament comes from the Greek word <u>charis</u>, which means "favor, blessing, or kindness."

We can all extend grace to others, but when the word grace is used in connection with God, it takes on a more powerful meaning. Grace is God choosing to bless us rather than curse us, as our sin deserves. It is His benevolence to the undeserving.

Ephesians 2:8 says, "For by grace are you saved, through faith, and that not of yourselves." *The only way any of us can enter into a relationship with God is because of His grace toward us.*

Grace began in the Garden of Eden when God killed an animal to cover the sin of Adam and Eve (Genesis 3:21). He could have killed the first humans right then for their disobedience. But rather than destroy them, He made a way for them to be right with Him. That pattern of grace continued throughout the Old Testament when God instituted blood sacrifices as a means to atone for sinful men. It was not the physical blood of those sacrifices, per se, that cleansed sinners; it was the grace of God that forgave those who trusted in Him (Hebrews 10:4; Genesis 15:6). Sinful men showed their faith by offering the sacrifices that God required. ("What is the Grace of God?").

Grace is so big for a Christian as we are no longer under the law. We live under grace, and that is what all of Romans is about. So I would love to say I am free. And I am!! Yay. Does that mean I can do whatever I want? Well, I will put it in Paul's words:

> **[1] ... *What shall we say, then? Shall we go on sinning so that grace may increase? [2] By no means! We are those who have died to sin; how can we live in it any longer? ...***
> **Romans 6:1-2 (NIV)**

When I finally understood what Paul was talking about, I wondered why I had not been raised this way. Why had I not been taught grace when growing up? Why was I brought up under the law? I felt robbed of a freedom I had never known.

I had also run from the Lord for years because of sin that had been in my life I felt He couldn't forgive me for. But under grace, maybe my life would have been different. So I went to my parents and asked them why they raised me under the law. This was how they felt was the best way to raise children. Teaching them right and wrong. Also, this was how they had been raised.

When I left, I turned and said, "Well, it's not how I will be raising my children!"

I remember my mom saying, "Well, we will see how that turns out for you."

Often out of fear, we can shy away from wanting to teach the truth of grace. However, I know how the Spirit works in me. And if the Spirit is alive in them, they will not get away with anything.

Now that is the biggest question. Is the Spirit alive in them? Did they give their life to the Lord? I can't answer that question. If they haven't, then they aren't saved anyway, and there is no amount of commandments I can teach them that will help them live *a holier than thou* life. I love raising my children knowing who the Lord is and how He came to die for them so they don't have to be perfect and so they can have a Helper. And hopefully, they cannot feel defeated in life. I pray they have the Spirit alive in them.

Is the Spirit alive in you?

Does the Spirit speak to you?

Do you want the Spirit to be in you?

Do you want to give your life to the Lord?

If the answer is yes, I pray that you ask Him to come into your life right now and to forgive you of your past sins. You can name them. And put them away! Meaning stop doing them. And if you are going to have trouble stopping them, don't worry, the Spirit will help you! He will come in and help take over if you want Him to be Lord of your life. So if this is your desire, for Him to come into your life and for Him to be Lord of it, then ask Him to come in and help you! He loves you! He is there to help you!

Now after experiencing my newfound freedom, I began my new journey of being free to obey. Freedom from this law that once bound me, and finding I was no longer bound to the law, once I had the Spirit in me who led me. I chuckle as I have come full circle. And oh, what a miraculous journey it has been!

Do I have to obey? Of course, I don't. But what I shared in the previous chapter is the blessings I miss out on, and the love my husband has for me gets squashed when I don't obey. So it is my choice. *And don't I want to be loved? Isn't that the ultimate desire of a woman?* Oh my, if she only knew the power she held in her hand by simply obeying. Oh, but that crazy curse blinds us from our blessings. Don't let that curse win out on your blessing!

Chapter 10 - Bible Study Questions

A) Growing up, (if you were saved before) were you brought up under the law. Were you taught to live by the law? What I mean by that is that when you sinned, you were told to ask for forgiveness and not taught you had already been forgiven for the sin before committing the sin.

1. Can you recall a time when you sinned and you now carry that guilt?

B) Sometimes when we sin and we feel we cannot be forgiven for that sin. We will turn away from God. Even hate Him for it, just because we don't understand what He has done for us.

1. Have you ever been in that situation?

2. Maybe you're in that situation. Does this help you to understand the love and forgiveness He has waiting for you?

3. Does this bring any freedom to your heart?

C) This verse was life-changing for me:

> *[21] I do not set aside the grace of God, for if righteousness could be gained through the law, Christ died for nothing!*
> Galatians 2:21 (NIV)

1. Can you explain why your righteousness could not be gained through the law?

2. Can you be perfect in everything you do?

3. Are you thankful for this Scripture? After admitting to not being perfect.

D) As a Christian, the sin is forgiven already at the cross. We are called to confess our sins and to acknowledge our sins before the Lord. To agree with the Holy Spirit that what we did was a sin. So often, when I do something wrong, the Holy Spirit says that wasn't right. And what I say is I know. I'm sorry. Now I am in agreement with the Holy Spirit.

1. At which age did you understand this principle?

2. How did it change your life?

3. How did it affect your walk with the Lord?

E) Often out of fear, we can shy away from wanting to teach the truth of grace.

1. How do you feel about this statement?

2. Do you teach grace or teach the law?

F) Are you saved? Do you know Jesus as your personal Lord and Savior? These questions might help determine the answer.

1. Is the Spirit alive in you?

2. Does the Spirit speak to you?

3. Do you want the Spirit to be in you?

4. Do you want to give your life to the Lord?

Chapter 11
Our Ultimate Happiness

The word happiness doesn't show up in the Bible too often, but when it does it talks about sharing in the Lord's happiness. Strangely through obedience:

> *[26] To the person who pleases him, God gives wisdom, knowledge and <u>happiness</u>, but to the sinner he gives the task of gathering and storing up wealth to hand it over to the one who pleases God. This too is meaningless, a chasing after the wind.*
> **Ecclesiastes 2:26 (NIV)**

> *[3] But may the righteous be glad and rejoice before God; may they be <u>happy and joyful</u>.*
> **Psalm 68:3 (NIV)**

> *[21] His master replied, "Well done, good and faithful servant! You have been faithful with a few things; I will put you in charge of many things. Come and share your <u>happiness</u>."*
> **Matthew 25:21 (NIV)**

[11] He has made everything beautiful in its time. He has also set eternity in the human heart; yet no one can fathom what God has done from beginning to end. [12] I know that there is nothing better for people than to be <u>happy</u> and to do good while they live.
Ecclesiastes 3:11-12 (NIV)

Our ultimate happiness comes from our obedience to the Lord. Not from our partner. But through our submission to the Lord.

There is nothing more miserable than being in a bad marriage. It is lonely, difficult, seems hopeless and forever. And who wants to live forever in a hopeless situation. As a Christian, all we can do is cry out to God. But likely all the signs of the bad marriage were there before we got married. We just didn't pay attention.

So I guess the question is… is there hope? There is always hope. Mostly because if we can step into our role and let the Lord fix our hearts then He can change the heart of our spouse.

Does that change in our spouse happen immediately? Ummmm, well, we are not God or our spouse. But I can tell you if it took ten years to change your spouse into a man of God then the next twenty years with him would be awesome! And the Lord sees you, and He loves you, and you can rest in that. He wants you to be happy, so be obedient in the situation you are in with the Lord, knowing He will bless you in your growth.

How can I say my happiness comes from my obedience to the Lord? Well, when trying to please the Lord we grow spiritually. We read our Bibles. Learn Scripture. Pray about our situations. Pray for understanding. And all while we are growing spiritually and we begin to understand the Lord and His design in our lives.

How much He loves us! This understanding of the love He has for us brings contentment and joy. We begin to be calm and at ease with our surroundings. Knowing that our God is in control at all times. Without this understanding, we are the opposite...scared and searching for outside comfort.

I know that marriage is difficult. I have been in a difficult marriage. So I try to remember that as I write some of my stories. I try to remember the hopelessness I felt and how you may feel.

I want to give you hope in the Lord, though. Give everything to Him. Submit your life to Him! He can heal your marriage. I can't promise a healed marriage, but what I can promise is when you submit your life to the Lord it is no longer yours to fail! He can do with it as He pleases. And if you are submitting yourself to your husband like you are to the Lord then it will make things much more difficult for him to treat you in an unloving way!

But maintaining that respect and treatment toward your husband will be your hardest feat. It cannot just be an act of kindness for some time but a change of heart. Find time to talk to him about what you are trying to do and have him help you be accountable.

You might think you want to surprise him with your actions to see if his actions change. However, you fall back into some old ways of doing things, and you're both back to being as you were. He would not understand you're trying to change. There would be no way to be excited about the process. So honestly, I don't think that would be the best idea.

Involve your husband in this change. Have him be your accountability partner. He is the best accountability partner you could have. He is the one you are accountable to besides the Lord. You can ask him if he has noticed changes. And if he thinks you could do better. Be ready; you might not want to hear the answer. But maybe it's great, and you're improving daily.

If he is an unsaved partner he will likely not understand this newfound desire to submit yourself to the Lord so find an accountability partner outside the home who you can talk to. Not a man! Another woman who can help you and counsel you along the way. However, even though he is unsaved, he would still be good to talk to and let him know what you are attempting to do. Every man wants to be respected.

Wow, I could never have imagined the blessings I received in my marriage. I am thankful every day for my amazing husband and best friend. But I can tell you for certain, I never tried to leave my first marriage, and I didn't try to go into a second one. So, relax and let the Lord be in control. He can take care of you. Trying to find a husband is when we make more of a mess.

Chapter 11 - Bible Study Questions

A) When the word happiness shows up in the Bible, it talks about sharing in the Lord's happiness through obedience.

1. Have you ever thought of those two words being significantly related to each other?

2. Why do you think being obedient to the Lord would lead to sharing in His happiness?

B) Our ultimate happiness comes from our obedience to the Lord. Not from our partner. But through our submission to the Lord.

1. Are you trying to seek your happiness from your husband?

2. Do you see how individuals can affect how we feel daily?

3. Is there a way you can focus on seeking the Lord and leaning on him solely for your happiness?

C) Marriages don't always work out how we think they are going to. So, is there hope? There is always hope. Mostly because if we can step into our role and let the Lord fix our hearts, then He can change the heart of our spouse.

1. What steps will you take today to step into your role to change your marriage?

2. How will you stay focused on your role and the Lord, not your husband and his faults?

D) God loves us! This love brings contentment and happiness. We begin to be calm and at ease with our surroundings. Knowing that our God is in control at all times.

1. Are you scared and lonely when you aren't focused on the Lord?

2. Do you understand that if you keep your focus on the Lord and His love then whatever happens, He will be there through it?

3. Do you know how much He loves you?

E) You might want to surprise your husband with your actions to see if his actions change. However, you might fall back into some old ways of doing things. He would not understand you're trying to change.

1. What changes are you going to make in the way you act with your husband?

2. Are you going to involve your husband in your life change?

3. How can your husband help you?

Chapter 12
Preparation

What are we doing? Well, that is the question, isn't it?

Here, we are married to our spouses and living under this curse of rebellion every day, and honestly, if we aren't working on getting out from under the curse, then we are likely getting worse.

Why is the Lord calling us to be under our husband's authority? Why wasn't I born a man and given that authority? I like authority. A lot!!

So what is going on?

What the Lord showed me is that we are preparing to go live with Him under His authority. WOW!!

And what was interesting is that I have no idea what He wants.

So I need to relax.

I am glad I wasn't born a man. There is so much responsibility on them. Women are constantly trying to take it off their hands. But now that the Lord has shown me this revelation, there are several reasons I'm glad I'm a woman:

I don't have to be responsible.

I don't even think women realize how much men feel responsible for and how much they are responsible for. Men put the responsibility on themselves, and God puts the responsibility on them. We, as wives, would be more supportive of our husbands if we understood this more. Therefore, maybe I can help to explain it a little bit.

A husband feels responsible for the safety of the family. When a wife comes into the marriage with an attitude of self-sufficiency and does not need a man, she has not considered that the man takes her safety as his responsibility. No matter how much she would love for him to consider her equal to him, he will always see a need to protect her. God created us this way and therefore gave him the deep desire to protect her. She needs to respect and understand this aspect of him as it is in his very nature.

Dennis Rainey, the President and CEO of FamilyLife, said it best on this subject, so I thought I would share what he said:

To borrow an illustration from John Piper and Wayne Grudem on the essence of masculinity: When you are lying in bed with your wife, and you hear the sound of a window being opened in your kitchen at 3 a.m., do you shake her awake and say, "The last time this occurred, I was the one who took our baseball bat and investigated to see if someone was breaking into our house. Now it's your turn, Sweetheart. Here's the bat!"?

No! That's when the man gets up. But being a protector calls for more than ensuring physical safety. Proverbs 4:10–15 describes a father who protects his son by passing on wisdom, helping him build godly character, and teaching him to reject the lies and temptations of the world. This father is protecting not only his son but also the generations to follow as the wisdom he shares gets passed on and on (Rainey, Dennis).

God puts the responsibility on the man of the decisions made in the family and home. Also, unless you are bucking him or changing those decisions, they are ultimately his decisions, and the accountability lies under him. We have talked about the man being under God and the wife then being under her husband. Hence she is protected by his decisions. This is a huge burden for a man to carry. I think sometimes we, as women, like to take it off of them. However, it is theirs to carry.

> **[23] *For the husband is the head of the wife as Christ is the head of the church, his body, of which he is the Savior.***
> **Ephesians 5:23 (NIV)**

Generally, a man feels responsible for making money in the home. They might find it more difficult finding a job, despite their willingness to work hard. When a woman makes more money than a man, then it can become burdensome and overwhelming to the man. Especially if he perceives she is judging him when he is not making as much as she is. He may find it more difficult to go to work because he feels defeated.

Remember to always be lifting your husband up regarding his job. I know that in today's society, many men are struggling even going to work, whether that is because the wife makes more money, because the wife's job moves and his job will be ever-changing, or because the wife is simply telling him he is not doing enough with words of non-affirmation. Honestly, there could be so many reasons a man struggles because he feels responsible. So understanding he feels responsible may help you to help him get going in the right direction and become his biggest supporter.

> **[8] *Anyone who does not provide for their relatives, and especially for their own household, has denied the faith and is worse than an unbeliever.***
> **1 Timothy 5:8 (NIV)**

Again, I found that Dennis Rainey said it well:

When a man doesn't work and provide for his family, he feels a sense of shame. His self-worth sinks. A man who doesn't work, who can't keep a job, who moves from job to job, or who refuses to assume his responsibility creates insecurity in his wife and children. Every man needs to provide for his family.

I find that most men feel a natural sense of responsibility in this area, but many don't seem to understand that providing for their family means more than meeting physical needs. It also means taking responsibility to provide for emotional and spiritual needs (Rainey, Dennis).

A man will feel responsible if the marriage is a failure. Notice, I didn't say if it is a success. They will only take on the failed portion of the marriage. I have seen some men walk away, and they did not feel they failed. However, there are three things to consider. The first one is are they a Christian, the second one is was it the first marriage, and the third is was there infidelity involved. Unfortunately, those three factors seem to play a role in whether the person walks away so easily. But a man feels ultimately responsible for the marriage.

I would like to add a caveat to that last statement. Almost all, whether they were Christian or whether it was their first marriage, would not walk away so easily from their marriage unless they were having an affair because they feel a responsibility to their marriage. However, I know they will not live in misery or perpetual disrespect.

I am so thankful for my husband, who can give me wisdom in this following paragraph. "To sum it all up, these men feel responsible because of their curse. As God put a curse on women affixed to their core; He likewise put a curse on men and affixed it to their core. So if they recognize their responsibilities given to them by their curse or not it is there. They are to toil the ground. Meaning to be responsible for working for their family and supporting them and taking care of them and providing for them."

We can see also that God calls men to provide for the family like Christ did the church, which is out of love to provide for them by loving it, working, sacrificing for it, nurturing it and to hold it accountable. In the end, Jesus is the leader of the church. Men can try to deny these inherent values or even run from them, but they will only be met by frustration and stress.

> *[25] Husbands, love your wives, just as Christ loved the church and gave himself up for her [26] to make her holy, cleansing her by the washing with water through the word, [27] and to present her to himself as a radiant church, without stain or wrinkle or any other blemish, but holy and blameless. [28] In this same way, husbands ought to love their wives as their own bodies. He who loves his wife loves himself. [29] After all, no one ever hated their own body, but they feed and care for their body, just as Christ does the church--- [30] for we are members of his body. [31] "For this reason a man will leave his father and mother and be united to his wife, and the two will become one flesh." [32] This is a profound mystery--- but I am talking about Christ and the church. [33] However, each one of you also must love his wife as he loves himself, and the wife must respect her husband.*
> **Ephesians 5:25-33 (NIV)**

I could only beg you to see the volume of stress that comes from the responsibilities involved and try to be the ultimate supporter of your husband.

When I think about it, *why am I a woman*? Had I been born a man, would I be humble? I don't think so. I struggle with it now. I wonder if I would have even been capable! I know the Lord would have made me perhaps the perfect helpmate to make it. And that's where I come in his plan. He must really love me to have put me right where he did! I feel I make the perfect helpmate! I'm so glad I'm not responsible for those other decisions.

It's interesting to think about how different men and women are.

My husband and I love watching the *Love and Respect* series marriage seminars. Dr. Emerson talks about men speaking through blue megaphones and women speaking through pink megaphones. He says if a man handed a woman a marriage book, the woman would be overwhelmed with joy thinking, *Oh my, he wants us to grow in our love*. Whereas, if a woman hands a man a marriage book, he thinks, *She thinks I'm not good enough*.

We definitely speak different languages.

However, in this case, I wonder what a woman would think if a man handed her this book and said, "I do care about our marriage, and here are my needs. Are you open to them?" Would the woman be receptive? I don't know.

Often, I think about the Bible talking about the Christian that is on milk and the Christian eating meat. There is a time when you could not have shown me these Scriptures. I would not have been receptive. There I was drinking milk. Many times the Lord keeps Scripture hidden from me, and when the time is right, it comes alive.

He will open it up to our eyes when we're ready to see it.

Every time you read it, He will reveal a new truth to you.

As I grow spiritually and I'm ready, He allows me to understand the next portion. Otherwise, it would be too much.

So often, I'm trying to feed that meat to women when I should feed them milk. I want others to be happy and know the peace and be at peace in their marriage. So, I hand them huge steak bites. But all too often, they haven't even had the baby food. They aren't ready, and we missed something.

The Lord opened my eyes at the right time. He fed me meat in the baby food jar. Then years later, after He showed me the love He had for me, He then brought me to understand how to be submissive. Maybe this was a little steak with potatoes. *Could I have been submissive without understanding grace? I would not have been as happy as I am today without the two going hand in hand.*

It is much harder to grow spiritually today than it might have been years ago. With so much going on in life, like television, video games, our cell phones and earbuds…and society teaching a different philosophy. It's difficult.

This is something to think about. When I think I have so much knowledge of the Scripture and that perhaps my husband is not spiritual enough, I need to remember that my knowledge of the Lord is not that grand. And if you think it is, let me share some Scripture with you…

Great is the Lord, and greatly to be praised, and his greatness is unsearchable.
Psalm 145:3 (ESV)

Behold, these are but the outskirts of his ways, and how small a whisper do we hear of him! But the thunder of his power who can understand?
Job 26:14 (ESV)

For my thoughts are not your thoughts, neither are your ways my ways, declares the Lord. For as the heavens are higher than the earth, so are my ways higher than your ways and my thoughts than your thoughts.
Isaiah 55:8–9 (ESV)

Oh, the depth of the riches and wisdom and knowledge of God! How unsearchable are his judgments and how inscrutable his ways! "For who has known the mind of the Lord, or who has been his counselor?"
Rom. 11:33–34; cf. Job 42:1–6; Ps. 139:6, 17–18; 147:5; Isa. 57:15; 1 Cor. 2:10–11; 1 Tim. 6:13–16 (NIV)

So my understanding was and is that one day I will be with Him and married to Him. Will I know how to act? Well, I'm practicing right now! I am under the authority right now!

Years ago, I went to visit my uncle taking care of my aunt at the nursing home. As a back story, my uncle got saved several years after marrying my aunt. I'm not sure if my aunt was saved or not. She may have been, and that is simply up to the Lord! She treated my uncle so badly and had treated him badly for years. I really couldn't understand why he stayed with her. She had been divorced six or seven times.

He would go see her at the nursing home, and she would throw things at him. She would tell people at the hospital and nursing home he would hurt her, so they would call adult protective services on him. Only to discover later that she was lying. He would always bring her food daily, every meal, even though food was provided. Because she had no teeth, he would grind her food up for her before he came.

I struggled to have any respect for him. I found that my mom and my uncle constantly made excuses for her actions. My mom would tell me, "Well, she lost her first child, and it was hard for her. Her first husband beat her up. She has never recovered from that marriage and not being loved."

Apparently, she loved her first husband, and when their first child was five years old, he was outside playing. Well, the neighbor's teenager had asked if he could back the car out of the driveway, and the parent said yes. But when he did, he ran over her son. She quickly grabbed her son, but instead of going to the hospital, she drove to her husband's work. He died, and the husband blamed her for the death.

When she got pregnant again, he beat her so badly she was forced to get false teeth, and she began to have seizures. He told her he didn't want her to have another child for her to kill.

There we were, fifty years later, and she could have behaved better. My uncle wasn't a Christian when he married her. I think he was 20 years old, and she was forty when they got married. Here she was at ninety, and I thought of all the years he had to live with her in that misery. I kept thinking, *Why would you live in misery like that?*

I had to know how someone could ever stay with someone like her. So one day when I went to visit them at the nursing home, I asked him why he stayed all these years.

She was sitting there in her wheelchair at the nursing home. He was sitting by her across from me.

I had so much disdain for my aunt I asked my uncle right in front of her, "Why, why do you do it?"

She had tried to have him arrested. If you walked in her home, she lived like a hoarder. He had to live in a fifth wheel outside the home. It was just too much for me. She would lie about him to everyone about things he did to her which were not true. They would figure out it wasn't true in time. But why?

"But why," he said. "When Jesus saved me and died on the cross for me He gave me everything. So when I look at her, I see Jesus, and I say to her, 'What can I get for you, and what can I do for you?'" He gets up in the morning, and he is with her. He makes her whatever food she wants. He comes to the nursing home and walks with her. He sits with her. He did anything and everything for her.

Oh my... my whole thought process and respect changed for him that day. What a man!! Wow! And did he ever teach me something! He told me that one day he would be with Jesus, and this was his practice. Additionally, if Jesus could die on the cross for him and give everything for him was there anything he wouldn't do for Jesus? Wow, to see Jesus in all that chaos and to say, "What can I do for you!" Amazing! Words cannot describe!

I know that my true desire is that I can practice every day right here and now for the day I am with Jesus. I pray I can see Jesus in my husband no matter what the circumstance and say, "What can I do for you?" I hope that I'm in good practice when my time comes to be with my Lord!

Chapter 12 – Bible Study Questions

A) We are preparing to go live with the Lord, under His authority.

1. Is this a new thought for you?

2. How does this make you feel?

B) I am glad I wasn't born a man. There is so much responsibility for them. Women are constantly trying to take it off their hands.

1. What are some things that men feel responsible for?

2. Did you understand before that men felt responsible for so many things?

C) It seems much harder to grow spiritually today than it might have been years ago with so much going on in life like television, video games, our cell phones and earbuds...and society teaching different philosophies.

1. What are distractions you have in your life?

2. What are changes you can make to get rid of those distractions?

D) So my understanding was and is that one day I will be with the Lord and married to Him.

1. What do you think it means to be married to the Lord?

2. Do you think this is exciting or scary?

3. How does this change your perspective on your marriage?

Chapter 13
Divorce

I wasn't going to write anything on this topic. However, I thought I should share my feelings. I do not believe in divorce.

You might ask, "How can you say that when you are divorced?"

Well, I have a hard time writing about my first marriage without feeling like I'm bashing my first husband. So, I don't want to do that. However, I want to write about how we tried to work it out so many times.

I told you before about getting pregnant when I was separated from him. But I didn't tell you that I moved back to the US while he remained overseas. Eventually, he came back, and we tried to work it out again. For seven years, we tried to make it work.

I can tell you in the seven years I was married, I likely lived with him for less than half of that time. When we lived together the longest period that we lived together was probably six to eight months. Then we would separate for at least a six-month to a year period, and we would repeat the process. We lived together less than the time we were separated.

If I told you he wasn't coming home at night after the first month of marriage, would that help you to understand how difficult it was?

After six years, I went to see a divorce lawyer, and I sat in his office, but I couldn't sign the papers. Even my divorce lawyer, a Christian, couldn't understand why I wouldn't move on.

We were separated, and everyone I knew supported me getting a divorce. However, I still felt that my marriage was under God.

My parents had constantly been telling me to remain in my marriage, thankfully. Eventually, my father sat me down and told me it was time to move on. It was the first time in six years.

Every time my husband left me, he would come back, and I felt obligated to reconcile. This happened often in the marriage. What was weird was at some point, I had absolutely no feelings for him. So I was reconciling with him solely because of my commitment to the Lord.

I remember when he finally came to leave and said, "It doesn't take a rocket scientist to tell you that you no longer want to be with me. I'm moving out." I was thinking, *Could I help you pack?*

When he finally left me, never to return, I finally felt released from the marriage. When I say never to return, I mean he left so often, it was always a question of whether he would come back or not. When he left, there was no anger, no resentment, no hostility. Everything had run its course. I think when you are angry, there are feelings, there is love, and when there is love, there is hope that was and is not being fulfilled. So whether there is hope or not, get back in there because the Lord can do amazing things. I'm a true testament to that.

There are several things to consider if you are in a rocky marriage and separation is involved. Always be ready to reconcile. Never be looking to have another relationship outside the marriage. Remain pure. You never know where your marriage will go. So you don't want to affect your marriage negatively. Try not to talk badly about your husband to others. Keep your conversations private and try to only discuss negative comments with a counselor. Ask the counselor if they think you should speak alone with them about some of these things, so you do not embarrass your spouse.

When my marriage finally ended, I never had to question whether I had given everything I had to the marriage. I had given everything, and I had always been available to reconcile. In the end, he got remarried and I was released from that marriage. However, I cannot express how much pressure it took off of me to know that I had given all I had. Even though I sometimes felt I had wasted years of my life. What years had it wasted? The Lord had the perfect guy waiting even years later for me. He was waiting for me to put myself together and give myself fully to him!

What to do when your husband mismanages money, cheats, lies, is slothful, slanders, has anger or abuse issues? I was asked this question recently. Remember that first off, you are not his Holy Spirit. Don't forget; you are not alone in your marriage. God is with you. You may feel alone, but this is not true. Anytime we come before God and make a vow, we have involved God in our lives. Now some people take that flippantly, and some don't. Which one will you be? Will you trust Him? Do you believe in Him? If you believe in Him, then you can allow it to fail. God deals with the husband, your marriage doesn't have to fail. Give him the freedom to fail. Let him learn from his mistakes. Give him room to breathe.

The other thing we must remember here is that I am not a counselor. I speak only from experience and from what the Spirit leads me to say. I deeply encourage anyone struggling to seek counseling. Additionally, if the husband won't go with you, then go by yourself. However, make sure you are seeking a good Christian biblical counselor, not just any counselor.

I started my second marriage, and I started it with no feelings. Now, this man and I are one. When the Lord said now you can date him, I struggled the whole time with letting go of the commitment I had made to the Lord to remain single and that He (God) would be my husband.

I remember my husband, while we were dating, asking me, "What was it going to take for you to commit yourself to me?"

I looked at him and said, "I guess just walking down the aisle and saying I do."

I think that so often, we can develop feelings when we let go and dream about the future with someone. However, I was not really free to do that as I had sincerely made a vow to God to remain single and had the Lord not spoken audibly, that would never have changed. So I struggled to let go of my vow and be obedient to that audible voice at the same time. It was a strange position that I had never been in before. Almost like an arranged marriage set up by God Himself. I think in arranged marriages, people are in the same position.

We have grown so much in our marriage. We have learned so much from each other. We love each other so much. We would die for each other. He is my rock and my greatest supporter. I can't imagine life without him. I thank the Lord every day for him.

There is hope even without feelings. You can fall in love with a man of God if you are fulfilling your role.

A friend called me once and told me she was getting a divorce. I asked her why. She told me because she had no feelings. I told her feelings come and go. I told her as a Christian, we needed to stay in our marriage and fight for our marriage and that we cannot base our marriage on feelings. This was over twenty years ago.

I enjoy looking at their pictures on Facebook together. They seem happy, and they have a great family. I would love to think that somehow I played a role in them staying together. But ultimately, she stayed with him, and as a Christian, she made the right decision. Her kids are grown now, and she and her husband seem to spend a lot of time together. I love her obvious devotion to the Lord and to her husband. Additionally, I know she has received a blessing for the time she has given to her marriage. What a great testimony she has that it can work!

What do you do if you have no feelings? Continue on living for the Lord. Doing for the Lord. Put it in His hands. Let Him be the driver. That is what I have had to do in my life. Let Him drive, and He will fulfill your life. If you try to control your life and where it goes, it will likely be a mess.

Feelings change depending on the circumstances surrounding you. Recently, we moved, and my senior started a new high school. He seemed to love the school until one day, he came home and told me how much he disliked the school. I really couldn't believe it. It bothered me so much. Had I moved him his senior year and destroyed his senior year?

When my husband came home from work, I talked to him about it, and he said he was fine until he got injured in basketball and couldn't play. I was relieved to realize that this was exactly the problem. Now I had to help my son to understand that this was the problem. Once I explained to him that his feelings weren't based on the school but on his circumstances, he became happier. I explained to him that the Lord knew he would be injured and gave the thumbs up that it was ok for that to happen.

We don't know why it happened but know that God always works for our best interest. He needed surgery, and hopefully, that will fix any future injuries from happening. He can move on and be better. He is a much happier kiddo looking forward to his future.

Understanding that your feelings can change by outside circumstances and affect other things in life is the first step to healing sometimes. Remember, if you are angry, there are feelings, where there are feelings, there is love, and where there is love, there is a deep desire, expectation and hope. Always be ready to reconcile. And even if there are no feelings, there is still hope. Serve the Lord. You can fall in love with a man if you are fulfilling your role.

Try to remember our God is a big God! He is in the business of reconciling. He wants our marriages to work as they are symbolic of His relationship with us. None of us are perfect! We all need Jesus' help for living with another person. But you are not alone. Jesus is there waiting to help you in whatever difficulties you might experience!

Chapter 13 - Bible Study Questions

A) The world today makes it easy to get a divorce! Have you heard that it is ok to get a divorce? Most people, Christian and non, wouldn't even think twice about it if you talked about getting a divorce.

1. How do you feel about divorce?

2. How do you think divorce affects the children?

3. Is there a time when you feel it is ok to get a divorce?

4. If yes? Can you support it with Scripture? Or is it man-made reasoning?

B) Being married has nothing to do with feelings, but it has everything to do with a commitment to the Lord. Committing your marriage to God is being ready to reconcile at any time when the husband is ready to reconcile, even when you have no feelings or desire to do so.

1. How hard would this be for you to do?

2. Do you understand the commitment to the marriage God asks of you?

3. Why do you think that marriage is not based on feelings?

C) If a spouse leaves you and does not return, then there is nothing you can do. Do not hold onto the guilt. If you have done everything to reconcile, let it go.

1. How can you be at peace in that area of your life if this happened to you?

2. How can you show compassion to someone else who is in this situation?

D) With anger, there are feelings, there is love, and where there is love there is hope that was and is not being fulfilled.

1. Do you see that if you didn't care about your spouse, you would not get angry?

2. Did you know there is a direct correlation between love and hate?

3. Did you know that anger can be selfish?

E) Keep your conversations private and try to only involve negative comments with a counselor not outside friends.

1. Are you one who talks to your friends about your spouse?

2. How has this chapter affected your thoughts on speaking to others about your spouse?

3. Are you keeping your husband's personal life a secret for him?

F) You never want to question whether you gave it your all.

1. What are you doing right now to give it your all?

2. What would you like to see change in the future that you need to pray about?

3. How could you change to be more effective in making that change happen?

Chapter 14
Listening to the Holy Spirit

Often people tell me that God isn't a God of Love, but a God of hate. With marriage, being in this submissive role could be taken that way.

We can see all of humanity played out in the women's role. When you are finally in the role you were meant to be in, the one God designed for you, then you will see things fall into place. This is not some worldly hierarchy based on whether one person is better than the other. Rather, the hierarchy is based on God's design. If one steps outside of God's design, marriage doesn't work.

If you want the puzzle pieces to fit and the picture to be perfect, then you fit in your place the way the Lord asks you to fit in your place. I understand that even saying this, may ruffle some women's feathers.

For men, God doesn't ask them to dominate the women with a fist. (I don't want to, nor am I, here to preach to a man. I am also not here to talk about this subject or to even interject much thought about it.) However, I want to put hope into a woman's heart. My husband says men are to love their wife like Christ loves the Church. I see Christ being patient, loving and guiding. He is the Shepard. He leads by example. He doesn't bully.

> *[25] Husbands, love your wives, just as Christ loved the church and gave himself up for her.*
> **Ephesians 5:25 (NIV)**

To the woman, I say STOP now and think, it can be easy to want to tell someone else their role and say, "Well, if you would do this, then I could do my role." My hope is for whoever is reading this to do your part. Play your role, and don't give up. Be like my uncle who, until my aunt's death bed, was practicing for his moment when he would be with the Lord, even though she was hateful until the end.

So it's not about your spouse. It's about the Lord. Get your focus off your spouse and put it on the Lord. Once you do this, then the Lord can work on your spouse and, believe it or not, on you.

All too often, we are reactive in our responses to our spouse. So everything we do is in response to what they do. Whether it is positive or negative.

This behavior doesn't bring healing to a relationship. What happens if your spouse has a bad day, a bad month, or has a long-term illness? Will you consistently respond to their pain with negativity? We give our spouse no allowances by being reactive.

So, the goal would be to break the habit of responding to our spouse based on his performance or actions or reactions. This is not an easy feat and takes Jesus' help.

The Holy Spirit can help us with this, but we must be careful not to drown out His corrections. Often, I am corrected by the Holy Spirit. I may be angry at the time and unwilling to listen to the Holy Spirit. So, I am disobedient to the Holy Spirit. Do you know this is a sin?

> *[19] Do not quench the Spirit.*
> **1 Thessalonians 5:19 (NIV)**

> *[30] And do not grieve the Holy Spirit of God, with whom you were sealed for the day of redemption. [31] Get rid of all bitterness, rage and anger, brawling and slander, along with every form of malice. [32] Be kind and compassionate to one another, forgiving each other, just as in Christ God forgave you.*
> **Ephesians 4:30-32 (NIV)**

Do you wonder how I hear the Holy Spirit? Maybe you have heard the Holy Spirit tell you not to do something. It's that still, small nudge or voice of correction that says, "That is not right." If you have not accepted Christ as Savior, then you wouldn't have Him. If you have accepted Him, then you have Him. Have you been quenching the Holy Spirit?

Let me try to explain it using an example:

"Imagine the Holy Spirit as a fire. When we quench the Holy Spirit, we are dampening God's flame instead of fanning it, pushing it down instead of helping it grow stronger and more beautiful" (Collins, Anna).

When the Bible talks about our sins being forgiven, it talks about us agreeing with the Holy Spirit when He brings those sins to mind. When He brings them up, I must agree with Him they are sin. Therefore, we agree that it is sin. But if I am not listening to the Holy Spirit, then we are no longer in agreement, and I am quenching the Holy Spirit. I am also grieving the Holy Spirit.

Although He desires for us to have the utmost humility, He is patient and very kind through our growing process. He waits for us to learn and loves us at whatever level we are on. It doesn't matter where we are, the Holy Spirit is always working to bring us closer to Him. His love will be displayed to others through us.

He cares deeply. He cares how we treat each other. He loves each one of us. His ultimate desire is for us to follow His example. If we could love each other and learn how to live together and be happy, He would be pleased.

However, we live in a fallen world. So, all we can do is fix ourselves and know that the Lord is real. He is in control. He loves you. He wants the best for you. So real change can only happen within ourselves. But real change can be effective and infectious.

[4] *A wife of noble character is her husband's crown, but a disgraceful wife is like decay in his bones.*
Proverbs 12:4 (NIV)

Be your husband's crown. I want your husband to want to love you and want to cherish you. To want to come home to you and spend time with you. I can't guarantee these things, but I can guarantee you will find freedom in the Lord. You will find that missing love you needed from your husband and receive it from the Lord. When you spend time with the Holy Spirit, growing with Him, spending time in the Word and making a decision that you're all in for the Lord, you can make Him number one and give Him your all.

Our ultimate happiness comes from the Lord. Our trust and obedience bring comfort and peace in our lives. We ultimately know that the Lord will take care of us if we are living according to His Word. Therefore, we can find peace in our lives, which brings happiness.

Chapter 14 - Bible Study Questions

A) We can see humanity played out in the woman's role. Everyone has to be submissive to someone. Man is submissive to God like we are to man, and it is a direct representation.

1. Do you see that being in a submissive role has been taken in a wrong way by women? Like God sees them as less?

2. Do you know of any women turned off by Christianity because of the submissive role that women are supposed to play?

3. Can you see how it works if there is someone in leadership? Can you also see it's not because you're of lesser value?

B) It can be easy to want to tell someone how they are supposed to be acting. And, in response, let them know that you could do what you are supposed to do if they held up on their end.

1. Why doesn't this work?

2. How will you combat telling your husband how they are supposed to be acting?

3. How will you look past how they are acting and look to the Lord for the Grace he pours out on you every day?

C) All too often, we are reactive in our responses to our spouse. So everything we do is in response to what they do whether it is positive or negative.

1. Think of a time when your spouse was in a bad mood, and you responded negatively to him?

2. Is there another time when you negatively reacted to a situation with your spouse because you were being reactive?

3. If your husband were in a bad mood, which one would work better for your spouse? To lift his spirits or to remain quiet?   If there is something else you could do to encourage him, then write it below.

D) I often think we are drowning out the Holy Spirit's corrections. And sometimes, if I'm angry enough, maybe I don't want to listen to the Holy Spirit.

1. Do you ever hear the Holy Spirit talk to you?

2. Do you ever drown out the Holy Spirit because of anger?

3. If yes. Do you know it's a sin?

4. Will you make a commitment to listen to the Holy Spirit?

Chapter 15
Women in History

Could Sarah have been unsubmissive in her days? Yes, women had a voice!

I feel I need to clarify a misunderstanding. I often hear people say times were different in the Bible and in the past. They claim women had no voice or women didn't hold high positions. However, the Bible says there is nothing new under the sun. I want you to know women have always wanted to be in charge:

[10] Is there anything of which one can say, "Look! This is something new"? It was here already, long ago; it was here before our time. [11] No one remembers the former generations, and even those yet to come will not be remembered by those who follow them.
Ecclesiastes 1:10-11 (NIV)

I thought I should bring to light stories to illustrate what I am talking about.

It is important to understand this because Sarah, by choice, followed her husband. By choice, she did not stand up to him and tell him no. I hope my stories can help you see that in history, women constantly did things that were wrong, and I promise I have only touched on a tiny surface of them.

I find it interesting that the Lord called me to homeschool my children from when my fourth child started first grade until he started high school.

For many years I had people tell me you should homeschool. I said, "No way! I can't stand to be around my kids. Haha." That's not really true. But I thought, *they barely listen so how can I homeschool them?*

When we moved to Florida, we could put my fifth child into Pre-K and the state paid for it. We didn't realize it was for them to basically pre-examine and decide if your child would go into regular class or special education class.

By the end of the year, the schoolteachers and counselors sat us down and informed us they thought he needed to attend special education. I thought, *no way*. My husband also thought the same way! My husband had never been on board with homeschool either, but it was the first time we were both reconsidering our options.

He was a quiet child, and I felt he would get lost in the crowd. I thought, *If he's in a Special Ed class and others demand attention, and he demands no attention... would he learn anything?*

We decided we should homeschool this child. As I pondered this new adventure, I thought, *How would it work to homeschool one child and all the rest go to school? How can I stop and deal with the rest of the kids and get them to school and then come back to him?* So we decided to just homeschool all four of our younger boys.

I called one of my best friends and asked her what curriculums she used. I looked at her children, and they were so intelligent, going to the best high schools after homeschooling, and doing well. I wanted that for my children.

Because there are so many curriculums out there for homeschooling, I needed somewhere to begin. I needed some idea of what courses to choose. So, we sat down and began a plan for the curriculum.

Little did I know that one curriculum that I would pick, with her direction, eventually led to reading some of the greatest books in history: *The Iliad* by Homer, *The Histories* by Herodotus, *The Odyssey* by Homer, *The Epic of Gilgamesh, Eusebius The Church History* by Paul L. Maier, *The Codes of Hammurabi and Moses* by Davies W. W., *The Aeneid* by Virgil, *Julius Caesar* by William Shakespeare, *The Last Days of Socrates* by Plato, *The Oresteia Trilogy* by Aeschylus, *Plutarch's Lives Volume 1* by Plutarch, *The Theban Trilogy* by Sophocles, *and The Twelve Caesars* by Suetonius. Plus an in-depth study of the Old Testament.

Having learned so much about History has helped me to know so much about the times in the past. I have learned about the women and who they were and how they acted.

As I began to write this book and hear what people have had to say about women and especially about Sarah's time, I think they miss the big picture. Women were not quiet. They were manipulative and sometimes downright evil.

Wow, have you read the story of the teenager who danced for the king and asked for John the Baptist's head on a platter? Salome was a young girl and was begged by the king to dance. He offered her anything if she would dance for him. Anything she asked? Anything! Thus, she danced for him and asked for the head of the prophet, John the Baptist.

Salome was the daughter of Herodias, the wife of Phillip the Tetrarch. However, Herodias was having an affair with Phillips' brother King Herod.

John the Baptist was vocal about their flaunting of their union being wrong and immoral. So Herodias had convinced her daughter to ask for John the Baptist's head on a platter.

[22] When the daughter of Herodias came in and danced, she pleased Herod and his dinner guests. The king said to the girl, "Ask me for anything you want, and I'll give it to you." [23] And he promised her with an oath, "Whatever you ask I will give you, up to half my kingdom." [24] She went out and said to her mother, "What shall I ask for?" "The head of John the Baptist," she answered. [25] At once the girl hurried in to the king with the request: "I want you to give me right now the head of John the Baptist on a platter." [26] The king was greatly distressed, but because of his oaths and his dinner guests, he did not want to refuse her. [27] So he immediately sent an executioner with orders to bring John's head. The man went, beheaded John in the prison.
Mark 6:22-27 (NIV)

Have you ever read the story Gyges and the plot of King Candaule's wife? The king was so proud of his wife and how beautiful she was. He bragged about her beauty. However, no one had ever seen her naked body.

As the story goes, he convinces Gyges to sneak into his chambers and wait for his wife to come in so he can see how beautiful her body is. He brought Gyges into the room and hid him there to wait until his wife came in. After a while, his wife came in and changed her clothes, and he saw her naked body. However, from the corner of her eye, she saw Gyges in the room. So what does his wife do when she sees Gyges out of the corner of her eyes? Nothing!

Later, though, she derives a plan. She corners Gyges and threatens him he has to kill the king (her husband) for doing such a terrible thing. Wait. What?! Who has to die? Why not have Gyges killed?

Seems that the king's wife had significant power here she shouldn't have, and not good power if you ask me. So, later the king's wife and Gyges are married, and Gyges becomes King of Lydia. *Hmmmm,* 680 BC - 648 BC. Honestly, it's thought they had a love affair long before, and this is the excuse she uses to get rid of her husband.

> *...again, the queen saw Gyges, but made no sign, as she understood the situation. Her love for Kandaules is therefore turned to hatred, and she dreams of revenge (uxorem-alienavit). Hence she yields to Gyges, who had fallen in love with her, and had therefore become the kings enemy (quo pacto-fecit). Not long after, having gained Gyges, she offered him the throne and herself if he would kill the king. The deed is accomplished and the price paid in full.*
> *(The Tale of Gyges and the King of Lydia)*

Let me direct you back to a biblical story you may know well about Abraham's cousin, Lot. His very own wife turned back and turned into a pillar of salt. Later, his two daughters had a whole different mission. They survived the flee of Sodom and Gomorrah. But after they fled, they both planned to get Lot, their own father, drunk so they could get pregnant. They thought every man just went up in flames in Sodom and Gomorrah. Especially their fiancés because they didn't heed the warning to flee. Hence, I guess they thought they better take things into their own hands.

[31] One day the older daughter said to the younger, "Our father is old, and there is no man around here to give us children---as is the custom all over the earth. [32] Let's get our father to drink wine and then sleep with him and preserve our family line through our father." [33] That night they got their father to drink wine, and the older daughter went in and slept with him. He was not aware of it when she lay down or when she got up. [34] The next day the older daughter said to the younger, "Last night I slept with my father. Let's get him to drink wine again tonight, and you go in and sleep with him so we can preserve our family line through our father." [35] So they got their father to drink wine that night also, and the younger daughter went in and slept with him. Again he was not aware of it when she lay down or when she got up. [36] So both of Lot's daughters became pregnant by their father.
Genesis 19:31-36 (NIV)

The prophet Hosea was told to marry a whore. She was a lover of the world. An example of us because we are the example of the whore. Again, this is another story in the Bible/history where we can see that not all women were submissive, quiet and good.

[2] When the Lord began to speak through Hosea, the Lord said to him, "Go, marry a promiscuous woman and have children with her, for like an adulterous wife this land is guilty of unfaithfulness to the Lord."
Hosea 1:2 (NIV)

Queen Jezebel, this ninth-century B.C. queen of Israel, was one of the most wicked women. Her life, as told in 1 and 2 Kings, was full of intrigue, sex, cruelty, and murder.

Jezebel is likely the wickedest woman in the Scriptures. She was strong-willed, politically shrewd, a murderer, and very fierce. She was a Phoenician princess who worshiped Baal, the pagan god of fertility. She marries King Ahab. She manipulates him to do whatever she wants him to do for her evil plans (Satchell, Michael).

[25] There was never anyone like Ahab, who sold himself to do evil in the eyes of the Lord, urged on by Jezebel his wife.
1 Kings 21:25 (NIV)

[13] Haven't you heard, my lord, what I did while Jezebel was killing the prophets of the Lord? I hid a hundred of the Lord's prophets in two caves, fifty in each, and supplied them with food and water.
1 Kings 18:13 (NIV)

[7] You are to destroy the house of Ahab your master, and I will avenge the blood of my servants the prophets and the blood of all the Lord's servants shed by Jezebel.
2 Kings 9:7 (NIV)

In the story of Sampson and Delilah - Sampson obviously loved Delilah but also didn't really trust her as he continued to not tell her where his strength came from. Delilah was being bribed by the Philistines with money to get information. So she was deceptive and manipulative. She continuously nagged and prodded him until he gave in. She was not the picture of a submissive or supportive woman.

As you can see in the next Scripture, he obviously loved her, and she used that love to get what she wanted out of him.

> *[15] Then she said to him, "How can you say, 'I love you,' when you won't confide in me? This is the third time you have made a fool of me and haven't told me the secret of your great strength." [16] With such nagging she prodded him day after day until he was sick to death of it. [17] So he told her everything. "No razor has ever been used on my head," he said, "because I have been a Nazirite dedicated to God from my mother's womb. If my head were shaved, my strength would leave me, and I would become as weak as any other man."*
> **Judges 16:15-17 (NIV)**

In the story of Joseph - Potiphar's wife was a great example of a woman with a lot of power, and she obviously had a lot of time on her hands. When nobody was around, she was with Joseph trying to get him to have sexual relations with her. She was definitely not being watched or controlled. And she was totally out of control.

Talk about a manipulative woman. Potiphar's wife throws herself on Joseph, and when he retreats quickly from her, she grabs his clothing off him, so she can frame him and say he touched her inappropriately. Joseph is sentenced to prison for a long time.

[6] So Potiphar left everything he had in Joseph's care; with Joseph in charge, he did not concern himself with anything except the food he ate. Now Joseph was well-built and handsome, [7] and after a while his master's wife took notice of Joseph and said, "Come to bed with me!"

[8] But he refused. "With me in charge," he told her, "my master does not concern himself with anything in the house; everything he owns he has entrusted to my care. [9] No one is greater in this house than I am. My master has withheld nothing from me except you, because you are his wife. How then could I do such a wicked thing and sin against God?" [10] And though she spoke to Joseph day after day, he refused to go to bed with her or even be with her.

[11] One day he went into the house to attend to his duties, and none of the household servants was inside. [12] She caught him by his cloak and said, "Come to bed with me!" He left his cloak in her hand and ran out of the house. [13] When she saw that he had left his cloak in her hand and had run out of the house, [14] she called her household servants. "Look," she said to them, "this Hebrew has been brought to us to make sport of us! He came in here to sleep with me, but I screamed. [15] When he heard me scream for help, he left his cloak beside me and ran out of the house." [16] She kept his cloak beside her until his master came home.

[17] Then she told him this story: "That Hebrew slave you brought us came to me to make sport of me. [18] But as soon as I screamed for help, he left his cloak beside me and ran out of the house."
Genesis 39:6-18 (NIV)

In the story of Jacob and Esau - Jacob's mother, Rebekah, asked Jacob to deceive his father, Isaac. Rebekah planned the whole deception out. Isaac sends the older son out and while he is hunting she sends Jacob to see his father Isaac to receive a blessing.

[5] Now Rebekah was listening as Isaac spoke to his son Esau. When Esau left for the open country to hunt game and bring it back, [6] Rebekah said to her son Jacob, "Look, I overheard your father say to your brother Esau, [7] 'Bring me some game and prepare me some tasty food to eat, so that I may give you my blessing in the presence of the Lord before I die.' [8] Now, my son, listen carefully and do what I tell you: [9] Go out to the flock and bring me two choice young goats, so I can prepare some tasty food for your father, just the way he likes it. [10] Then take it to your father to eat, so that he may give you his blessing before he dies."
Genesis 27:5-10 (NIV)

All the caveats we put on women in history, simply because we weren't there, are not true. We assume, because of laws of the past, that women must have been submissive. Women have always been smart and manipulative. However, outside of having to answer to God, you will find that women will act as badly as they can get away with.

Jesus spoke to the woman at the well. He saw her as a woman who had value. She meant something to Him. Even though she had been with so many men and not married to them. The woman at the well mattered to God. Jesus is the author of the Bible, and she was important. She had her own voice, so God took the time to talk to her directly. He wouldn't have talked to her if she were not important to Jesus.

[7] When a Samaritan woman came to draw water, Jesus said to her, "Will you give me a drink?" [8] (His disciples had gone into the town to buy food.) [9] The Samaritan woman said to him, "You are a Jew and I am a Samaritan woman. How can you ask me for a drink?" (For Jews do not associate with Samaritans.) [10] Jesus answered her, "If you knew the gift of God and who it is that asks you for a drink, you would have asked him and he would have given you living water." [11] "Sir," the woman said, "you have nothing to draw with and the well is deep. Where can you get this living water? [12] Are you greater than our father Jacob, who gave us the well and drank from it himself, as did also his sons and his livestock?"

[13] Jesus answered, "Everyone who drinks this water will be thirsty again, [14] but whoever drinks the water I give them will never thirst. Indeed, the water I give them will become in them a spring of water welling up to eternal life." [15] The woman said to him, "Sir, give me this water so that I won't get thirsty and have to keep coming here to draw water." [16] He told her, "Go, call your husband and come back." [17] "I have no husband," she replied. Jesus said to her, "You are right when you say you have no husband. [18] The fact is, you have had five husbands, and the man you now have is not your husband. What you have just said is quite true." [19] "Sir," the woman said, "I can see that you are a prophet."

[25] The woman said, "I know that Messiah" (called Christ) "is coming. When he comes, he will explain everything to us." [26] Then Jesus declared, "I, the one speaking to you---I am he."
John 4:7-19, 25-26 (NIV)

If people say that times were different and women were different than women are today, then they don't know their history. If they say that women's voices and opinions were or are of no value, then they don't know my Savior.

If women didn't matter, then why did Jesus care about women? Why did He spend so much time talking to the woman at the well? Jesus saw value in Mary and Martha as He spent much time with them.

There were a couple of times Mary (Jesus' mother) had a strong voice, and little was heard about Joseph. Usually, we only hear from Mary even when they turned back in search of Jesus to find Him teaching in the synagogues.

The Bible points to women having value and their voice and opinion being heard; so, an argument that the times were different and women had no value or no voice does not hold up, especially to Jesus.

I want to encourage you to know that you have value. Understand and know that you have strength in what you say. Combat your desire to control your husband. Even though we have value does not mean we need to devalue our husbands. If we give them deep respect, they will lift us up and see us as priceless.

Now, isn't that what we are seeking overall?

Chapter 15 - Bible Study Questions

A) I often hear people say times were different in the Bible and history, and women had no voice or women didn't hold high positions. The Bible says there is nothing new under the sun. Women have always wanted to be in charge.

1. Have you heard this before?

2. What were your thoughts going into this chapter?

B) Herodias was having an affair with the king and was angry that John the Baptist was vocal about it being wrong. So, she asked Salome, her daughter, to ask for his head when she was rewarded for dancing. The king was sad. When comparing today to this, I can't imagine that happening. I think we would have WW4. People would likely go nuts if this happened.

1. So put it into the perspective of today. Did women seem more submissive? What are your thoughts?

2. The king did not want to do this evil act but had made a promise of a gift up to half his kingdom to Salome. Was his girlfriend being submissive?

3. You already know she was someone else's wife, so you know she is not submissive to him either. What do you think she is teaching her daughter with this behavior?

C) I want to stick mostly with Scripture stories for our Bible study, so let's talk about Jezebel. She marries King Ahab and urges him to do evil, as the Bible says. The Bible says she was the one killing prophets.

1. Have you ever heard of Jezebel before?

2. What can you find out about Jezebel? Where did she come from?

3. Does Jezebel paint the picture of the old submissive woman?

4. Are you understanding that women have always been the same? Well, perhaps, maybe people were worse back then!

D) Delilah was an interesting character. A manipulative person. I can't imagine what was going on in her head. In my head I'm thinking, *Why not manipulate Sampson to marry you? Why go for the money?* Now don't get me wrong, the money seemed grand, and she was a prostitute. *But why not marry him and live in wealth? Because he could have had anything he wanted.*

1. Go back and read the story of Sampson. Judges 13-16 How devastating is the life of Sampson?

2. Interesting thought; what happened after the father interfered with the wedding?

3. Don't you think the money/payment would be fleeting but if she got Sampson in the end she could have whatever she wanted?

4. What would women in today's time do?

E) Potiphar's wife wanted Joseph and followed him around like a puppy dog. When no one was around she tried to get him to sleep with her. But when he retreated, she took his cloak. Then used it to say she took it off of him when she screamed, and he retreated. Wow, she is awful!

1. Can you imagine anyone setting someone up like this? She has to know he's going to prison for life! For no reason.

2. What example does Joseph set for us here, even or especially as women?

3. How can we be more like Joseph in our lives?

4. Write down what we all should learn from how Joseph responded to Potiphar's wife's evil plans.

E) When Rebekah asks Jacob to deceive her husband Isaac, it's because she loved Jacob more than Esau. So she develops a plan to help Jacob be better than Esau.

1. How does this affect Jacob (you may have to read the Scripture)?

2. How does this affect Esau?

3. How does this affect Jacob and Rebekah?

4. Would you say her deception was worth doing?

5. Does God fix everything in the end?

F) Jesus stopped and spent time with the woman at the well. She was surprised that he would even speak to her. He wanted her to know that she had worth! She had value!

1. Do you see Jesus giving value to the woman at the well by speaking to her?

2. Do you understand that being submissive is not to say you are less important or worthy?

3. What do you think God is doing by spending time with her?

4. Do you feel you have value?

Chapter 16
My Final Letter

Do you remember being in love for the first time? That first boyfriend? You would've done anything for him. He could have asked you to do anything.

I think that's how we are as wives. When we first get married we will do anything for our spouse. But as we become more familiar with him, as we live each day with him, we become less willing participants.

In the end, the spouse thinks, who is this woman? Who is this woman that I've married? She's nothing like the person I was dating. He acts a little less interested in the wife, and she feels less loved.

There's a great marriage series called *Love and Respect* that helps a couple to understand and combat this cycle by Dr. Emerson Eggerichs. It just talks about this cycle. It also talks about how this cycle repeats itself. Where he feels less respect and she feels less love (Eggerichs, Dr. Emerson and Eggerichs, Sarah).

The cycle is awful. It's hurtful. On both sides. I believe it starts with a growing familiarity in the marriage happening when a wife is not doing what she was doing initially because she's being less submissive.

The problem is we are called to respect our husbands. However, a wife does not understand what that word even means. When she hears it, it's just a word with no real meaning.

I find it interesting that men think that women know what it means. However, they don't ask a woman for the definition. If they asked the woman for the definition, they would be surprised to find that most women would give the definition that had something to do with love.

I want to clarify what it means. It means everything that I have talked about in this book. It means being a submissive wife. Being an obedient wife. Lifting your husband up with words of affirmation and never belittling them. Not because you have to, because certainly after you're married for a while, you don't want to, but because you want to be a submissive and encouraging wife.

You may have had some hard situations happen that caused you not to want to be submissive. You may even have been hurt. I want to urge you to seek counsel to try to resolve any problem or problems that have or could cause frustrations in your marriage. If there is a question of sin in the marriage, I would encourage you to seek counsel to resolve this issue. Sin in a marriage only leads to destruction.

I know that hurt in a relationship is by far one of the hardest things to overcome. However, how you respond to your husband, based on the knowledge you have received now, is what is important. It is what we are called to do and what we are called to be as Christians, to stand apart from all others, not to act the same as the world.

Therefore, just because the world acts a certain way doesn't mean we have to. We are called to be different and to act differently.

The same is true when we continue in our marriage. We are called to act differently. Perhaps to act like we did when we first dated our husbands.

Keep John's words close to heart. My mother calls it the formula for going back to where you started!

[4] But I have this complaint against you. You don't love me or each other as you did at first! [5] Look how far you have fallen! Turn back to me and do the works you did at first...
Revelation 2:4-5 (NLT)

As Christians, we should always seek a close relationship with our Lord. Ultimately this relationship should stir up a desire to be submissive to our Lord. So, be submissive to your husband because you want to be submissive to the Lord (Ephesians 5:22-24) and because you want all of the things that I told you about as far as the blessings go for your relationship.

Do you want that love that your man has to offer you? If you want that from him, then the only way you'll get it is by offering respect. This action is up to you. So, when you think about respect, think submissiveness. Think, obedience. Think about Sarah, who said, "Yes, Lord."

Now you have a choice; you can change your marriage or not. It's up to you to be obedient to the Lord. Everything is your decision to make. No one can force you to do it, and no one can prevent you from doing it. Also, no one can steal the gift that God will give you for doing your part.

Whether God's ultimate design is to heal your marriage or not, that's up to Him! Also, it's up to both partners. He's definitely not a God that forces any of us to do anything. But He will bless you in your obedience. So strive to be obedient to the Lord in your marriage, and I pray it is the best it can be. I pray you find the ultimate happiness in your marriage from being obedient to the Lord, like I have!

Chapter 16 - Bible Study Questions

A) When you were in love the first time, were you willing to go to a movie and a baseball game? Or sit with him while he watches a football game?

1. What does your husband want to do (activity-wise) that may not interest you? And when you dated, did you do it with him?

2. When you dated, did you go with him or sit with him and watch any sports or events?

3. Now that you're married, do you find it difficult to still sit with him and watch these sports or events?

4. Does your husband get frustrated when you don't want to join him, or does he go find someone else to enjoy it with?

B) I talked about a cycle where a man feels less respect from a woman, and she feels less loved. And both start acting on how they feel, and the cycle spins. He feels less respect, and she feels less love because of how they react to their behaviors.

1. Have you experienced this in your relationship?

2. Have you reacted to it?

3. How do you stop having a reactive relationship?

C) I don't think a wife understands what the word "respect" even means. When she hears it, it's just a word with no real meaning.

1. Did you know what respect meant?

2. Did you think of love when you thought of respect as the two being the same thing?

3. How can this change how you view your marriage?

D) We need to understand that respect is submissiveness and obedience.

1. Was this lesson a surprise to you?

2. How will this change how you interact with your husband?

3. Can you commit to being respectful even if it is only coming from you and not reciprocated?

E) Sometimes, past hurts in a relationship can affect how we respect our spouse. God calls us to be forgiving and still be under our spouse.

1. How difficult is this statement?

2. How can someone overcome past hurts

F) Revelation 2:4-5 (NLT) says, *"But I have this complaint against you. You don't love me or each other as you did at first! Look how far you have fallen! Turn back to me and do the works you did at first. If you don't repent, I will come and remove your lampstand from its place among the churches."*

1. How does this speak to you about returning to how we treated our spouse in the beginning?

2. Have you committed your marriage to the Lord? What will it take for you to commit your marriage to the Lord?

3. Can you pledge to focus on the Lord and serve Him through your husband?

4. Write a prayer asking the Lord to stir up a desire to be submissive to your husband. Pray for your husband's love to be overflowing in response to your submissiveness. Pray that the two of you are blessed beyond measure with God's peace and love.

G) The Holy Spirit spoke to me about getting on my knees before my husband (this was not literal but figurative).

1. How do you think the Spirit was leading me?

2. What action can you make to begin this process (I wanted to come back to this question from the first chapter)?

Epilogue

This book is not for the faint at heart, for sure. Most would and will have a problem with my not addressing men leading women into sin and women standing against it. I know that I'm going to catch some flak for it. But this is not my book, it is the Lord's. I have to remember that. I didn't want to write it! So while I wrote the book, I had to ensure it was from the Holy Spirit and matches Scripture.

Therefore, when you can find Scripture that says women should go against what their husband tells them, we can sit down and talk. And I'm not talking about a few Scriptures put together here and there that you can interpret to mean maybe that's what she should do. Again we are operating out of fear.

I know that my God is a big God and he will not play if a man is willingly taking an unwilling partner through sin! I believe you should continue in prayer for your partner and pray to God for his leadership and direction. I am only here to lead you to do what is right, and the Holy Spirit will direct that path! I guess what I have been led by the Spirit to say is that most don't believe God will intervene as he did for Sarah. So they are fearful and want the wife to stand against the husband. Leaving her always in judgment of her husband's actions and requests.

I am saying that if our God is a big God then He will protect us if we are obedient to our husbands and He will intervene on our behalf and take care of the situation at hand. So being in prayer at all times would be the most important part of our lives. But again, do we believe? Have we seen God in action? Do we believe He will come to our rescue? I think it depends on prayer, fasting, and the true desire of Him to intervene on our behalf. But what do I know.... I only speak from a little experience. And I know that when I seek, the Lord comes to my aid. So I know He listens. Do you believe? Well, I guess that's the question.

[13] You will seek me and find me when you seek me with all your heart.
Jeremiah 29:13 (NIV)

I would love to say I never mentioned standing against your husband with sin in my book from the beginning, but I would be lying. I actually had things in there but was led to remove them. I cannot, in good conscience and with the guidance of the Holy Spirit, tell a woman to tell her husband no in regard to anything. I have no idea if he is looking out for her safety or not. But she should be in prayer at all times and seek counsel regarding anything she feels that is sinful in the marriage.

I am not a counselor and will not pretend to be one. I hope you understand I am writing this book to a woman who lives under a Christian husband, who I assume is living under God! If a woman is living under a non-Christian husband, then she is called to try to live with him in peace if at all possible.

[13] And if a woman has a husband who is not a believer and he is willing to live with her, she must not divorce him. [14] For the unbelieving husband has been sanctified through his wife, and the unbelieving wife has been sanctified through her believing husband. Otherwise your children would be unclean, but as it is, they are holy. [15] But if the unbeliever leaves, let it be so. The brother or the sister is not bound in such circumstances; God has called us to live in peace. [16] How do you know, wife, whether you will save your husband? Or, how do you know, husband, whether you will save your wife?
1 Corinthians 7:13-16 (NIV)

I pray this book brings you great peace and success in your marriage. My prayer is that you have every desire to seek the Lord and His obedience in your life. I pray the Lord blesses your marriage.

Until we meet again.

Acknowledgements

I want to acknowledge those that were in my life that so lovingly spurred me on to lead a Bible study. My sincere thanks to Shirley Newcomb, Jennifer Craddock, Lori Jens, Tina Schneiderwent, Shawna Kruschke. These were my original Women's Bible study group, from Sheboygan. They've encouraged me to continue to seek the Lord and guide women to live in submission under their husband.

To our best friends that always walk beside us, Tim and Jackie Arnoldi. Thank you for your guidance in our lives.

My sincere thanks to the two women who pushed me to write the book. No doubt from the leading of the Holy Spirit. Thank you, for letting Him lead you, to tell me to write this book. Thank you A.C. Babbitt and Melissa Walczak.

Thank you to several of my beta readers for their help in reading and finding several mistakes in my book beforehand: Jessica Bowe, Bill Brummett, and Analyn Stokes, Michael and Gigi Elliott, Melanie DeVriend, Shawna Kruschke, Shirley Newcomb, Barbara Lock, Darrin Connor.

A special thank you to my Uncle, Arthur James Glennon, who still probably doesn't know how much of an impact he made on my life.

Thank you to my mom, Ruth Minton, who taught me by example.

I want to express my deepest gratitude to my husband, Greg Taylor, who worked tirelessly with me, to help me make the book the best it can be.

Finally, I want to express a deep gratitude to my daughter, Amber Rodgers, who has helped me tremendously with this book.

Sources

1. Collins, Anna. "Are you Silencing the Holy Spirit?" NewSpring Church: Copyright 2023. https://newspring.cc/articles/why-dont-i-hear-the-holy-spirit. Accessed 2023.
2. Copperman, Dr. Alan. "What Your Cervical Position Tells You About Your Fertility": Progony.com. (https://progyny.com/education/trying-to-conceive/cervical-position-fertility/). Accessed 2023.
3. Edgar, Bill, Dr. Geneva College Board of Trustees Member and Former President. "The Wise Woman Builds Her House…" 3 October 2016. https://www.geneva.edu/blog/biblical-wisdom/proverbs-14-1. Accessed 2023.
4. Eggerichs, Dr. Emerson and Eggerichs, Sarah. "Love & Respect Conference and 10 Week Study Couple's Kit." Conference DVD recordings: 1999.
5. Hermann, Ray, D.Min. "Abram's Sister-Wife: How Sarai Become Part of Pharaoh's Harem." 2 July 2020. https://outlawbiblestudent.org/abrams-sister-wife-how-sarai-become-part-of-pharaohs-harem/. Accessed 2023. Article quote cited Borgman, Paul, Genesis: The Story We Haven't Heard, (Downers Grove, IL: IVP Academic, 2001), pp. 42–43.
6. Mazokopakis, Elias E. and Samonis, George. "Is Vaginal Sexual Intercourse Permitted during Menstruation? A Biblical (Christian) and Medical Approach." Maedica (Bucur). 2018 Sep; 13(3): 183–188. Greek. doi: 10.26574/maedica.2018.13.3.183. (https://www.ncbi.nlm.nih.gov/pmc/articles/PMC6290188/#!po=40.3226). Accessed 2023.

7. Rainey, Dennis. "5 Ways Men Need to Step Up as Husbands and Fathers." Adapted by permission from Dennis Rainey's book, Stepping Up: A Call to Courageous Manhood, 2011, FamilyLife Publishing. FamilyLife: A Cru Ministry, 2023.
https://www.familylife.com/articles/topics/life-issues/relationships/men/5-ways-men-need-to-step-up-as-husbands-and-fathers/. Accessed 2023.
8. Satchell, Michael. "Jezebel was a Killer and Prostitute, but She had Her Good Side." USnews.com: 25 January 2008. https://www.usnews.com/news/religion/articles/2008/01/25/jezebel-was-a-killer-and-prostitute-but-she-had-her-good-side. Accessed 2023.
9. Scripture quotations are from the ESV® Bible (The Holy Bible, English Standard Version®), copyright © 2001 by Crossway, a publishing ministry of Good News Publishers. Used with permission. All rights reserved.
10. Scripture quotations marked (NIV) are taken from the Holy Bible, New International Version®, NIV®. Copyright © 1973, 1978, 1984, 2011 by Biblica, Inc.™ Used by permission of Zondervan. All rights reserved worldwide. www. zondervan.com The "NIV" and "New International Version" are trademarks registered in the United States Patent and Trademark Office by Biblica, Inc.™
11. Scripture quotations marked "NKJV" are taken from the New King James Version. Copyright © 1982 by Thomas Nelson, Inc. Used by permission. All rights reserved. Bible text from the New King James Version® is not to be reproduced in copies or otherwise by any means except as permitted in writing by Thomas Nelson, Inc., Attn: Bible Rights and Permissions, P.O. Box 141000, Nashville, TN 37214-1000.
http://www.nelsonbibles.com/

12. Scripture quotations marked (NLT) are taken from the Holy Bible, New Living Translation, copyright © 1996, 2004, 2007 by Tyndale House Foundation. Used by permission of Tyndale House Publishers, Inc., Carol Stream, Illinois 60188. All rights reserved. http://www.newlivingtranslation.com/ http://www.tyndale.com
13. Slattery, Dr. Juli. "Do Wives Always Have to Say Yes to Sex?: Why Healthy Interdependence in Marriage is the Key to Mutual Sexual Satisfaction." Today's Christian Woman: October 2015 Issue. (https://www.todayschristianwoman.com/articles/2015/october/do-wives-always-have-to-say-yes-to-sex.html). Accessed 2023.
14. The Tale of Gyges and the King of Lydia. Author(s): Kirby Flower Smith Source: "The American Journal of Philology" PDF, 1902, Vol. 23, No. 4 (1902), pp. 361-387 Published by: The Johns Hopkins University Press Stable. URL: https://www.jstor.org/stable/288700. Accessed 2023.
15. Urban, J. Kristen. "Isaac and Ishmael: Opportunities for Peace within Religious Narrative": Journal of Religion, Conflict, and Peace, Copyright 2013. (http://www.religionconflictpeace.org/volume-2-issue-2-spring-2009/isaac-and-ishmael)." Accessed 2023.
16. "What is the Grace of God?" Gotquestions.org. 4 January 2022. https://www.gotquestions.org/grace-of-God.html. Accessed 2023.
17. Zoromski, Kevin. "How Men and Fathers Express Emotions." Michigan State University, MSU Extension, 4 March 2018.

About the Author

Ginger Taylor is a Christian author, cosmetologist and instructor, stay-at-home and homeschool mom, professional musician, and avid advocate for healthy marriages.

Growing up, Ginger spent her summers working at the Gano Mission Center, as the youngest summer missionary, beginning at age 14, with Mildred McWhorter, the well-known founder of missions centers in Houston, TX.

Ginger grew up singing professionally with her family, known as the "Minton Family."

She loves leading children's plays at church. She enjoys speaking and teaching, leading women to learn how to follow their husbands.

Ginger is a wife and a mother of seven children. She was a business owner of a salon that made "Top One Hundred Best Salons in America" in *Elle Magazine*, in the July 2010 edition: (https://www.elle.com/beauty/hair/tips/a2478/united-states-of-style/). It was featured in *American Salon* magazine in the September 2010 issue, and listed in *Brides* magazine, as one of the best salons for wedding hair and makeup, in the August-September 2014 issue. She quit working to stay home with her four youngest children and homeschool them, until they were in high school.

Ginger graduated from San Jacinto Junior College with her associate degree. She continued her education to become an instructor in Cosmetology. She enjoys sewing, crafts, playing bridge and playing games with her family. She loves going on trips with her family and enjoys cruises.

Her goal is to inspire each woman to be actively seeking to become the woman God has called her to be and to discover how to become a "godly wife."

Website: authorgingertaylor.com

Instagram: @authorgingertaylor

Facebook: @authorgingertaylor